MW00806752

"Dr. Kullman gives us a superbly detailed and profoundly insightful account of eating disorders, forms they take, structures and roots. She covers a lot of ground with depth and wisdom. It is a book steeped in experience, at once clinically useful and highly creative, with much to offer a wide variety of readers."

— **Michael Eigen, Ph.D.**, *author of* The Sensitive Self, Contact With the Depths, *and* Birth of Experience

"Alitta Kullman has accomplished a somewhat remarkable feat. Drawing on forty years of clinical experience with hundreds of eating disordered patients, she has managed to write a text that is both accessible to practitioners who are new to working with this population and relevant to those with many years of experience. Her writing is clear and compelling, and she does a masterful job of integrating cutting edge theory with vivid clinical examples. Whether you are looking for a singular definitive volume on working with patients who struggle with food or are seeking to add to your existing library on eating disorders, you will want to own *Hunger for Connection*."

— **Steven Kuchuck**, *Editor*, Clinical Implications of the Psychoanalyst's Life Experience: When the Personal Becomes Professional, *and President-Elect, International Association for Relational Psychoanalysis and Psychotherapy (IARPP)*

"Dr. Kullman addresses eating disorders from a standpoint of sensitivity, knowledge, and experience. Hunger for Connection offers a clear and comprehensive appreciation of the roots of eating disorders in the emotional context of the earliest feeding relationship. It is beautifully presented and detailed, and reflects her own unique understandings and experiences. She combines compassion with theoretical and clinical sophistication to elucidate the interpersonal complexities and communications that are conveyed when the basic process of eating is disturbed. Her formulations are intricate, elegant, and offered in a manner that is accessible, engaging, and exciting."

— **Naomi Rucker, Ph.D.**, *Psychologist and Psychoanalyst, co-author of* Subject Relations: Unconscious Experience and Relational Psychoanalysis

"*Hunger for Connection* made me hungry for more of Kullman's informative and innovative ideas about how food obsessions replace thinking as a way to manage life's many ups and downs. As someone who has tried many diets over the years, I followed Dr. Kullman's patients' efforts to manage their eating disorders with great interest—especially how their therapist used both their relationship and their unearthing of long-buried family conflicts to change their lives. As a practicing psychoanalyst I found Dr. Kullman's positive approach to a wide range of eating disorders clinically helpful, illuminating, and eminently readable."

         – **Justin A Frank, MD**, *Psychiatrist and Psychoanalyst*

"As a psychoanalyst and psychologist specializing in Eating Disorders myself, I have known about Dr. Alitta Kullman's work since her article first appeared in the professional journal, 'Psychoanalytic Dialogues.' I have often referred to her article as I struggle to understand my own eating disorder patients. I eagerly look forward to being able to use her book as a reference for my patients, and hope it will soon be in print."

         – *Janet K. Smith, Ph.D.*, *Psychologist and Psychoanalyst*

"As a psychologist specializing in Eating and Body Image Disorders, I find Dr. Alitta Kullman's writing to be unusually innovative and engaging. She ties together in a uniquely engrossing style clinical and theoretical ideas about the 'perseverant' personality, a phrase she coined, which so aptly describes a core dynamic of eating disordered patients. Alitta is bound to write a gripping book, which I look forward to sharing with my patients, supervision groups and other professional colleagues."

         – **Judith Ruskay Rabinor, Ph.D.**,
*Psychologist, author of* A Starving Madness: Tales of
Hunger, Hope, and Healing in Psychotherapy

"I just finished reading your published article on the 'perseverant' personality, and I just wanted to say thank you. I have never read anything that has been more accurate in depicting what my internal world is really like. Your theory was spot on in every dimension. I can't wait to show my therapist...I hope you continue your work as I will look for anything you publish, for it has given me much hope."

         – **Marissa**, *message to the author via Psychology Today*

# Hunger for Connection

WHO DEVELOPS WHICH EATING DISORDER AND WHY? When do eating disorders begin and what fuels them? In *Hunger for Connection*, psychoanalyst and eating-disorder specialist Alitta Kullman expands on the 'body/mind' personality organization she calls the 'perseverant personality', illustrating how food and thought are linked from infancy, and for some, may become the primary source of nurturance and thought-processing for a lifetime—leading to what we call an eating disorder.

Kullman introduces nearly a dozen innovative terms to the psychological literature that help capture and give new meaning to the solitary, cyclical, or 'perseverant' eating and thinking patterns of bulimia, binge-eating disorder, and 'yo-yo' binge/dieting—explaining how and why they differ from what she calls the 'restrictor' disorders of anorexia, orthorexia, and chronic obesity. She builds her case by way of engaging illustrations of her interactions with patients, combining her relational psychoanalytic perspective with meditative and cognitive-behavioral strategies to propose the 'both/and' treatment approach she calls 'un-covery'.

Writing in a highly accessible style, Kullman offers an essential guide to understanding and working with cyclical eating disorders of all types. From psychoanalysts, psychotherapists, and counsellors, to eating disorder specialists, researchers, and students, *Hunger for Connection* not only provides guidelines for therapists of varying theoretical orientations and levels of expertise, but help and hope to people who suffer with eating disorders and those who care for and about them.

**Alitta Kullman**, Ph.D, Psy.D, LMFT is a psychoanalyst and psychotherapist in private practice in Newport Beach, CA. She specializes in the treatment of people with eating disorders.

# Hunger for Connection

## Finding Meaning in Eating Disorders

*Alitta Kullman*

Routledge
Taylor & Francis Group
LONDON AND NEW YORK

First published 2018
by Routledge
2 Park Square, Milton Park, Abingdon, Oxon OX14 4RN

and by Routledge
711 Third Avenue, New York, NY 10017

*Routledge is an imprint of the Taylor & Francis Group, an informa business*

© 2018 Alitta Kullman

The right of Alitta Kullman to be identified as author of this work has been
asserted by her in accordance with sections 77 and 78 of the Copyright,
Designs and Patents Act 1988.

All rights reserved. No part of this book may be reprinted or
reproduced or utilised in any form or by any electronic, mechanical,
or other means, now known or hereafter invented, including photocopying
and recording, or in any information storage or retrieval system,
without permission in writing from the publishers.

*Trademark notice*: Product or corporate names may be trademarks
or registered trademarks, and are used only for identification
and explanation without intent to infringe.

*British Library Cataloguing in Publication Data*
A catalogue record for this book is available from the British Library

*Library of Congress Cataloging in Publication Data*
Names: Kullman, Alitta, 1946– author.
Title: Hunger for connection : finding meaning in eating disorders / Alitta Kullman.
Description: Abingdon, Oxon ; New York, NY : Routledge, 2018. |
Includes bibliographical references and index.
Identifiers: LCCN 2017037908 (print) | LCCN 2017038619 (ebook) |
ISBN 9781315267111 (Master) | ISBN 9781351972093 (Web PDF) |
ISBN 9781351972086 ( ePub) | ISBN 9781351972079 (Mobipocket/Kindle) |
ISBN 9781138289581 (hardback : alk. paper) | ISBN 9781138289604 (pbk. :
alk. paper) | ISBN 9781315267111 (ebk)
Subjects: | MESH: Feeding and Eating Disorders—psychology
Classification: LCC RC552.E18 (ebook) | LCC RC552.E18 (print) | NLM WM 175 |
DDC 616.85/260651—dc23
LC record available at https://lccn.loc.gov/2017037908

ISBN: 978-1-138-28958-1 (hbk)
ISBN: 978-1-138-28960-4 (pbk)
ISBN: 978-1-315-26711-1 (ebk)

Typeset in Bembo and Gill Sans
by Florence Production Ltd, Stoodleigh, Devon, UK

This book expands and draws upon an article first published as Kullman, A. (2007)
The 'perseverant' personality: A pre-attachment perspective on the etiology and
evolution of binge/purge eating disorders', *Psychoanalytic Dialogues* 17(5): 705–732.
Reprinted by permission of Taylor & Francis, LLC.

*For Uri*

# contents

# prologue

THE INSISTENT SHRIEKING OF THE ALARM clock came as a relief. Megan didn't know how long she had been lying there, numb, frozen, since she had awakened again, terrified, long before dawn. She couldn't remember when thoughts of the legal brief she had to complete by Thursday had been replaced by fears of the court appearance she had scheduled for Friday. Nor could she recall when she first realized that the night that had just passed was not unlike so many others since she and Jon had been married, just two months before: She had gone to bed early and Jon had not come upstairs.

*Jon must be mad at me*, she shuddered, panic rising in her throat. *He must know. He has to know. How could he not know?*

Megan reached for her phone and entered Jon's private number.

"Hi, Meg!" he responded warmly. "I didn't want to wake you. How are you?"

"Oh, I'm fine," she lied, trying to keep her voice steady. "I was just a little worried that you didn't come to bed again last night. Is everything okay?"

"Hey, I'm really sorry, Meg," Jon apologized. "I fell asleep on the couch. I was up till 2:00 a.m. prepping for my deposition this morning. Are you really okay, Meg?"

"Yes, really, I'm really okay," she tried to reassure him. "Don't worry about me. Just have a good day. I love you."

Megan set her phone down on the nightstand, relief tainted by sadness.

*I am such a fraud*, she sighed. *I have to get better. I just have to get better. It's not fair to Jon.*

Megan pulled the quilt over her head and closed her eyes. She wished she could call her mother, but Mother wasn't speaking to her again. Megan knew the ritual well: She had to wait until her mother started missing her and found some excuse to call. If she called her mother first, she risked hearing what a disappointing and selfish daughter she had turned out to be. Besides, she couldn't tell her mother the truth anyway.

"Enough!" she ordered herself, casting off the covers. "Today will be a better day!"

Megan eased out of bed, trying to ignore the aching in what felt like every inch of her emaciated body. Staring intently at her image in the full-length mirror, she lifted her shirt and turned sideways to see how far her stomach was sticking out this morning.

*Not too bad*, she decided, her mood lifting. *Maybe I'll wear my new yellow suit and walk to the office.*

She stepped on the bathroom scale.

"Oh my God!" she exclaimed in horror. "How did that happen?"

Suddenly, Megan felt fat covering her body. She stared in the mirror again, critically assessing the indentations at her hip bones, wondering how she had missed noticing how fat she was just moments before.

*I was sure I got everything up yesterday*, she calculated, trying to control her panic. *And I didn't eat a thing after 4:00 p.m.!*

"You can't go out like this," she berated her image in the mirror. "You can't be seen like this. You need to stay home and work on your brief and just have coffee. You can't eat a single thing!"

Megan gathered her laptop and cellphone from the bedside table and headed down the stairs, her mind already taking mental inventory of the contents of the refrigerator, freezer, and pantry. Abandoning her devices on the dining room table, she hurried into the kitchen, filled a pot with water and set it on the stove to boil for pasta. She popped four pieces of bread into the toaster, pulled a carton of eggs from the refrigerator, and poured a cup of milk to heat in the microwave. Then, ripping open the box of sugared cereal she kept hidden in the pantry, she filled her mouth with grainy sweetness and exhaled with momentary relief. When the microwave sounded its four familiar beeps, she replaced the cup of milk with a frozen dinner she found in the back of the freezer, and poured the milk over a large bowl of cereal, sucking in its soothing warmth.

Megan binged for exactly one hour, thoughts of Jon and her mother and worries about the legal brief she must complete all weaving in and around the shame and remorse she felt for failing to keep yet another pledge to herself. Then, her stomach filled beyond capacity, she purged until she tasted bile and forced herself through a punishing regimen of exercise before taking several laxative tablets, "just to make sure." The familiar emptiness in her gut provided her with a few precious moments of relief. But as she tried to focus on her work, the need to eat became so consuming, the whole cycle began again.

Three binge/purge cycles, a ten-mile run, and a trip to the grocery store later, Megan surveyed the kitchen for any telltale signs of its ravaging as she waited for Jon to return home. Freshly showered, she felt better, cleaner, relieved in the knowledge that her body would remain empty for the rest of the day.

Jon arrived on schedule, and wrapped his arms around her.

"How are you doing?" he asked, pulling her towards him. "You wouldn't believe what a day I've had!"

"Really?" Megan brightened. "What happened?"

"Well, after the deposition I got this call from. . . . Hey, wait a minute!" Jon interrupted himself, holding Megan out at arm's length. "You've gotten so damn thin, Meg! You're like skin and bones! What's going on with you?"

Megan froze, momentarily unable to speak. "Nothing," she mumbled, "I'm fine, really. It's just stress. I've had this brief to write and . . ."

Jon reached for Megan's hand and led her to the sofa, pulling her onto his lap.

"I don't think this is just stress," he said, concern lining his brow. "You never eat a thing anymore at dinner, but then I know you eat a lot over the weekends. I don't get it."

Megan's cheeks flushed and she buried her head in Jon's shoulder, hoping he wouldn't notice.

"Look," Jon insisted, "I know I've been really preoccupied lately, Meg. There's been so much going on at the office. I know I haven't been paying enough attention to us."

Megan lifted her head and looked at him with a mix of curiosity and concern.

"What's been going on at the office?" she asked.

But Jon wasn't backing off this time.

"Seriously, Meg, let's not change the subject. I really want you to get some help. I know you don't like to talk about it, but . . ."

"No, no," Megan interrupted, Jon's concern piercing her protective barrier, "I know you're right. I've had a referral for a long time. I'll call tomorrow. I promise."

# *introduction*

THE PEOPLE WHO SIT IN MY OFFICE for the first time have been through it all. They have been on every diet known to humankind. They know the calorie counts, carbohydrate and fat grams of every conceivable edible substance. Many have been hospitalized for so-called 'purging anorexia' or bulimia, been through multiple courses of therapy, tried twelve-step programs. Some are frightened, devastated by years of failure, despairing of who and how they are. Others are skeptical: Nothing else has worked, they might say or imply. Why should I believe you?

You shouldn't, I tell them. This isn't about believing *me*. It's about believing *you*. It's about taking seriously the pain and sadness that brought you here and seeing how *together* we can make sense of it.

I have never met anyone with an eating disorder whose story didn't make sense to me. In the more than forty years I have been practicing psychotherapy (including twenty as a psychoanalyst), treating hundreds of patients with eating disorders, I have come to believe that eating disorders are eminently logical: Food is there when no one else is. Food helps when no one else can. Food is protection, comfort, presence in the dark of day or night. How can you give up the only thing you can count on?

Yet every day, millions of people caught up in cyclical eating disorders try and do exactly that. They wake up each morning promising themselves to end their tortured relationships with food. They vow to be 'good', to eat only vegetables, to resist all temptations. But when their planned regimens collide with the emotions that overwhelm their minds, the promises disintegrate: "*Something happens*," and within a fraction of a second, their resolve disappears. It is as if they literally 'lose their minds', unable to recall why they should do anything but eat foods they just seconds before had no thought of, or hunger for. Whether they then binge and purge multiple times a day, or gain and lose the same weight over and over again, the minds of people with cyclical eating disorders are on a merry-go-round. They turn to food over and over again for reasons having little to do with feeding the nutritional needs of their bodies, but then seek ways to eliminate what they've taken in. The same food they need with a fierceness that transcends their ability to *think* in one moment, turns toxic and perilous in the next. The need to get food *out* of their bodies—by purging, using laxatives, engaging in excessive exercise, or starving in order to lose weight—soon becomes as urgent as was the need to take it in.[1]

Cyclical eating disorders affect as many men as women, as many children as adults. People who binge and purge (or binge/diet), have been both breast-fed and bottle-fed as infants; they have had working and stay-at-home moms. They have achieved outstanding academic and professional successes, and they have been dogged by learning disabilities. They come from every socio-economic group, race, creed, and color. They have had fat parents and thin parents. They have been raised with pride and with prejudice.

So, what is the common thread? How is it that people growing up with such diverse backgrounds manifest almost identical patterns when it comes to their relationships with food? Speak to any one of them and they describe hauntingly similar thought processes surrounding their binges and similar sets of rituals surrounding their diets or purges. They speak of gnawing hunger, of incessant 'food thoughts', of vicious self-hatred, of shame. Whether they weigh eighty pounds, or many times more than that, their despair is couched in fear of eating or being 'fat', of craving foods that are 'dangerous', of having others see them, or *not* see them, as they are.

Yet despite these similarities, people with binge/purge eating disorders have been diagnosed with every form of psychopathology, their enactments attributed to failures at every stage of psychological development. Indeed, there is little agreement among eating disorder professionals and researchers as to how and why these particular symptoms develop and what perpetuates them.[2] As an unfortunate consequence, therapists often find themselves without a clear sense of whom or what they are treating, and patients continue to be misdiagnosed and/or remain without an understanding of, or long-term relief from, their persistent symptoms. And as eating disorders spiral into epidemic proportions in all segments of the population, critical questions remain unanswered:

- Who develops which eating disorder and why?
- When do eating disorders begin and what fuels them?

- Why does this particular set of symptoms develop as opposed to some other?
- What differentiates the *thinking* in one eating disorder from another?
- How do cyclical eating disorders become a reasonable choice and a logical conclusion for those who suffer them?
- What are the implications of all this for treatment?

*Hunger for Connection: Finding Meaning in Eating Disorders* unravels the intricate relationship between the *physical enactments* of cyclical eating disorders and the circular and distressed *thinking* that underlies them. Moving beyond the traditional 'multi-dimensional' or 'no-one-knows-what-causes-them' models, it demonstrates how the seeds for an eating disorder are sown virtually from the beginning of life, how they can be tracked and predicted from infancy, and how every thinking and eating pattern associated with them can be explained. Showing how nature and nurture intersect in forming early thinking and eating patterns, it illustrates how even *unintentional* emotional misattunements (if left unrepaired) can result in food becoming the primary source of emotional nurturance for a lifetime, laying the foundation for an eating disorder and creating vulnerability for later-developing psychological conditions that may accompany it.

In *Hunger for Connection*, I expand on the ideas first conceived in my doctoral dissertation and later published as "The 'perseverant' personality: A pre-attachment perspective on the etiology and evolution of binge/purge eating disorders" in the journal *Psychoanalytic Dialogues* (2007).[3] I define the **'perseverant personality'** as "a solitary and circular mode of being, thinking, and relating that is organized around a sustained physical and emotional reliance on the feeding as a means of thought processing and emotional regulation."[4] In essence, people with perseverant personalities learn to '*think*' with their bodies; their bodies and minds work *interchangeably*, rather than *interactively*. Emotional experiences that overwhelm their minds persistently trigger involuntary physical responses—'food thoughts', cravings, urges to starve or purge, faulty body images—rather than the thought-based solutions they really need to help soothe and regulate their emotional states.[5] In as literal a sense as we can muster, people with perseverant personalities use *food for thought*.

*Hunger for Connection* is built on a relational psychoanalytic model—influenced in particular by the thoughts about the origins of thinking developed by psychoanalyst W. R. Bion, M.D.—that integrates body and mind and illustrates how early developmental experiences and relationships impact the way we learn to think, eat, and ultimately, self-regulate. The symptoms and enactments of an eating disorder are viewed as metaphors, each one symbolizing thoughts, ideas, and feelings for which words have not developed or cannot describe. Family history and dynamics are explored—not for the purpose of ascribing blame—but in the service of understanding how they play a role in the formation of personality, and how they may inadvertently set the stage for 'thinking' with the body rather than the mind.

*Hunger for Connection* is organized around *composite portraits* of my clinical work with eating disorder patients, highlighting what I believe to be consistent and/or universal themes in people who suffer with cyclical binge/purge eating disorders and the perseverant personality organization they share. Toward this end, each chapter and vignette not only *tells* about an element of the perseverant personality, but shows how that element manifests within the individual and within the context of the therapeutic alliance. At every juncture, *Hunger for Connection* goes beyond *what* the perseverant individual is doing and asks *why?* Why this particular symptom or enactment? Why now? How is this individual trying to help him/herself?

Part One, *Making the connection*, is about beginnings: Beginning with Megan, a new patient reaching out for help, it illustrates how the ideas for the perseverant personality first came into being. It integrates psychoanalytic theory, psychoneurobiological research, and my own clinical experience to show how "uncontained"[6] emotional interactions that begin with the earliest feedings can influence the development of thinking, lay the groundwork for the perseverant personality, and ultimately foster the development of a cyclical eating disorder.

Part Two, *'Thinking' with the body*, introduces the perseverant personality organization and highlights its individual components. It shows how these elements work together to establish a distinctive psychological framework in which cyclical binge/purge eating disorders thrive and impact the every-day lives of individuals who suffer them.

Part Three, *Thinking with the mind*, integrates my contemporary psychoanalytic perspective on the treatment of eating disorders with meditative and cognitive-behavioral strategies to illustrate the 'both/and' approach I call **'un-covery'**. Arguing that traditional symptom-management protocols often teach patients to 're-*cover*'—or '*cover-up*' unresolved emotional issues again and again—'un-covery' combines strategies to offer what I believe to be a more targeted, inclusive, and effective model for the treatment of eating disorders than any single model might achieve on its own. Demonstrating how an eating disorder is a powerful blueprint to the psyche of a perseverant individual, Part Three also explores challenges that inevitably arise in the course of treatment and celebrates successes that enrich the lives of patients on their roads toward 'un-covery'.

A few notes on process. Throughout the text:

- I use the terms 'mother' or 'other' or a combination of the two—(m)other —to connote the primary caregiver/feeder, be they male or female.
- I use feminine pronouns most frequently. This reflects the greater number of female patients I have worked with, but in no way is intended to imply that the perseverant personality is limited to the female gender.
- I use the term 'patient' as opposed to 'client', as I believe it better captures the emotional state of the individual seeking relief from a distressful condition.

The perseverant personality organization may be unique among diagnostic classifications in that it does not embrace pejorative medical, disease, or addiction models. It does not look to what is 'wrong' with people, but rather to the ways in which creative, resourceful, sensitive, and perceptive individuals learn to contain their own anxieties and disruptive emotional states by substituting their own body-based capacities to manage them. In *Hunger for Connection*, I argue that we bring to life's table what we are served, but ultimately must decide what to take and keep in. By reconsidering and reframing the past and experimenting with new emotional 'cuisines', I hope to show how perseverant individuals can confront the automatic patterning in their brains, de-link and differentiate food from thought, and re-channel the *perseverant* patterns that feed their eating disorders into the *perseverance* to live a more nourishing life.

## Notes

1 Kullman, A. (2007). The 'perseverant' personality: A pre-attachment perspective on the etiology and evolution of binge-purge eating disorders. *Psychoanalytic Dialogues* 17(5): 705–732, 707.
2 Ibid., p. 705.
3 Ibid., pp. 705–732.
4 Ibid., p. 718.
5 Ibid., p. 720.
6 Bion, W. R. (1962b). Learning from experience. In *Seven Servants: Four Works by Wilfred R. Bion*. Northvale, NJ: Jason Aronson, 1977, pp. 1–111.

# Part one

# Making the connection

# *reaching for connection*

"I JUST CAN'T LIVE THIS WAY anymore," Megan said to me in a barely audible whisper. "My whole life circulates around my eating disorder. I can't go anywhere without making sure I have access to a bathroom so I can throw up. I can't wait for my husband Jon to leave in the morning so I can binge. Lately, he's been getting suspicious. I just don't know what I'm going to do."

The image of Megan's face on the day she began her therapy is etched in my memory. Tall and slender, with long dark hair, porcelain skin, and pale glistening lips, Megan's eyes exuded a mixture of warmth and terror that instantly captivated my attention as they latched onto mine. Meeting for the first time in the waiting room of my office, Megan extended her hand in greeting, the warmth of her manner belying the fear in her eyes. But, as she settled herself on the couch and began telling me about herself, it quickly became apparent that her demeanor had been carefully crafted to conceal a lifetime of pain.

"I was always the fat girl," Megan's voice quivered, her façade already threatening to crumble. "I remember weighing sixty pounds when I was just six years old and hearing the pediatrician tell my mother that I was 'just too fat'. I was mortified. After that, my mother started watching everything I ate. My brothers could eat anything they wanted, but anything *I* put into my mouth—from a celery stick to a spoonful of ice-cream—got analyzed or commented on in some way."

I nodded, encouraging her to go on.

"I know *now* that my mother was totally obsessed with her own weight, and that my father put a lot of pressure on her for us both to be thin. But *then*, it was like living under a microscope. By the time I was nine, my mother was carting me from one diet doctor to another, to weight-loss clinics, even hypnotherapy. But in between the diets and the promises, I couldn't ever stop thinking about food." She sighed deeply. " I guess I learned really early how to hide things from everyone."

Megan reached for a tissue and blotted the tears beginning to streak her makeup. "They never understood what it was like for me," she whispered when she could speak again. "How humiliating it was to have other kids make fun of me or not want me on their team. How I felt like my Dad only loved me if I was thin or losing weight. If I cried because I was being teased, my mother would tell me to ignore it. 'You're just too sensitive, Megan', she would say. 'Just start eating healthy and everything will be fine'. Or she would stare at me with that 'look' in her eyes and say, 'You have such a beautiful face, Megan. Why can't you just try a little harder?' But no matter how hard I tried, no matter how many promises I made to myself or to her or my father that *this time* would be different, every diet ended with me weighing more than before."

By the time she turned thirteen, standing five-foot-six inches tall and unhappily overweight, Megan determined never again to suffer the humiliation of being called 'fat'. She carefully constructed a six-hundred calorie diet and refused to budge from her prescribed plan. Before long, she became a "walking fat-and-calorie-counter," refusing to take in even an ounce of fat. She scrutinized nutritional labels, studying the exact composition of every food she even considered eating. Soon, almost no food felt safe. She cut her lettuce leaves and cucumbers into tiny bits and pieces; she mixed her small packet of oatmeal with two cups of water and left most of it in the bowl.

"Why are you so stubborn?" her mother now argued. "Why won't you eat?"

Megan was hospitalized in an eating disorder treatment unit when she was fifteen, weighing less than eighty pounds. But soon after her release, she began having difficulty maintaining the strict diet she still tried to adhere to, and her hunger, long kept under wraps, erupted. At first, she would stop for a candy bar or hot chocolate at the convenience store on her way home from school. But those secret encounters with chocolate soon turned into massive binges. On weekends, she would wait for everyone to leave the house so she could melt into the bags of food she kept hidden in her closet. She could eat a dozen eggs at a time, followed by six pieces of toast and three bowls of cereal. Then, when she could take in no more, she would purge until she tasted bile, the physical emptiness providing familiar relief.

"I felt like I was caught in a vise," Megan said intently. "I needed the food so desperately I can't even begin to describe it. But I couldn't *bear* the thought of being fat again."

Bingeing and purging seemed like her only way out.

As college loomed on the horizon, Megan felt a mix of emotions. On the one hand, she couldn't wait to get out from under her parents' constant scrutiny; on the other, she was afraid to leave. Being away from home had always terrified her. She felt so unsure of herself, so used to being told what to do and how and when to do it, she was afraid she wouldn't be able to manage on her own. But, finally bolstered by an academic scholarship, a new wardrobe, and assurances that she could come home whenever she wanted, Megan took off for her father's ivy-league alma mater. Schoolwork hit like an avalanche. Her professors expected her to *think*, she told me, and it seemed as if they all wanted her to do it on the same night. Megan could barely get through a sentence in her textbooks without grabbing for her stash of candy or eating an entire bag of popcorn. Her frequent trips to the bathroom to purge began irritating her roommate, and soon there was a strained silence between the two. Megan called her mother every night and begged to come home. At first it was just for a weekend, but then she pleaded with her mother to let her leave school.

"Just pull yourself together, Megan," her mother insisted. "It's almost winter break. Just hold on. You'll be fine!"

Her father wasn't much help either.

"You have a brilliant mind, Megan," he said somberly. "You are carrying on our family tradition. I know how disappointed you will be in yourself if you let this opportunity get away from you."

Megan sank deeper into despair. She became increasingly isolated and dependent on her binges to get her through the endless days and nights. But, despite her purging, she began to gain weight. By winter break she had doubled the "freshman fifteen," leaving her bursting out of her new college wardrobe and living in sweats. Home for the holidays, she once again tried to avoid her father's scrutinizing glances and her mother's nutritional advice. Concerned about her weight gain, her parents urged her to get back into therapy when she returned to school—something she had refused to do after her hospital experience. But Megan felt that her college counseling center therapist "just didn't get her," and she was uncomfortable with sharing in the group setting. Convinced that she just needed to have "more willpower" and work harder at overcoming her eating disorder by herself, she moved into a single room and returned to the bulimia and isolation that by then had become an integral part of her life.

Megan managed to complete college with honors and graduate three years later at the top of her law school class. Her parents beamed with pride on graduation day and bragged to their friends that they were looking at the future managing partner of her father's prestigious law firm. Even her weight seemed to have stabilized, with Megan assuring her parents that anorexia and bulimia were long buried in her past. She had passed the Bar and was working as a Junior Associate at her father's law firm when she met Jon, a young, politically-ambitious constitutional lawyer. Their wedding had been the social event of the season.

But neither Jon nor anyone else knew the terrible secret Megan still closely harbored: That her bulimia was indeed far from dead and buried. In fact, she still felt like she needed it to keep her alive. Megan knew that Jon suspected and was terrified he would leave her instantly if he knew the extent of her bingeing and purging. But, try as she might, she could not interrupt the cycle on her own. Megan was desperate: How could she continue to hide the truth from Jon? What would she do if he found out?

"Have you considered letting Jon in on your struggle?" I asked gently, waiting for her tears to subside.

"I've thought about it," she replied. "But I'm scared to. What if he doesn't understand? What if he's repulsed? I couldn't blame him. I *am* repulsive."

I looked at this beautiful, accomplished young woman hunched over on my couch, cowering in shame. How hard she had worked to keep herself hidden, to keep from being exposed. How convinced she was that anyone who really knew who or how she was would inevitably reject or abandon her.

"What makes you think Jon would find you repulsive?" I asked quietly.

Megan looked at me incredulously. "Do you have any idea what I *look like* when I'm eating?" she asked. "Or what it's *like* to hang over a toilet half your life?"

"I think I have a pretty good idea," I replied. "But I'm not nearly as concerned about what you look like on the *outside* in those moments as I am about what's happening with you on the *inside*. It seems to me that there's an awful lot of sadness and hunger all tied up inside you that you feel you have to deal with alone."

Megan looked away, tears again trickling down her face.

"I don't know why I am so self-destructive," she whispered, hiding her face in her hands.

"I know that's the way it may appear, Megan," I said softly, noting how quickly she had turned her anguish against herself. "And I know a lot of people might see it that way. But to my mind, your bulimia isn't a way you are trying to *hurt* yourself or anyone else. You obviously have experienced quite a lot of pain in your lifetime. Why would you intentionally try and inflict even more? The only thing that makes any sense is that, in some very meaningful way, you are trying to *help* yourself by bingeing and purging. It will be our job to make sense of it together."

Megan was relieved to learn that I was not about to hand her a "'ten-point program' for recovery." Her bulimia was far more than a bad habit I expected her to break in thirty days or less. I had seen far too many people invest their own (or their parents') life-savings in eating disorder recovery programs, only to be emotionally devastated when they returned to 'real life' and fell back into their old patterns. I explained that the work I do is not short-term, nor would it reap instant results:

"Therapy for me is not a food plan or a set of 'techniques'," I said candidly. "It is about helping you *un-cover* how and why bingeing and purging has become the way you process your emotions. Our work together will be about helping you learn to think about and manage your feelings with your mind instead of your body; to make choices that come from the *inside* of you rather than from the *outside*."

Megan nodded in agreement. She'd had enough of trying to "white-knuckle" a recovery, she told me.

Finalizing the arrangements for our work together, I was relieved to learn that Megan had recently confided in her medical doctor, who had checked her heart and blood pressure and ordered a panel of blood tests. Her health, it appeared, was still holding up. Nor did I need harp on the dangers of severe purging with Megan. She told me herself she knew she was playing Russian roulette with her life.

★   ★   ★

Peering into the inner world of an eating disorder, the uninitiated might see only the obvious. They would see people like Megan, eating with uncontrolled urgency, ingesting thousands of calories in a single sitting. They would observe her rituals of bingeing and purging, her compulsive exercise, her physical and verbal self-abuse. From the outside looking in, eating disorders defy understanding. But from the inside looking out, every enactment conveys a profound message: Every binge is an act of desperation; every purge or bout of starvation an effort at managing the thoughts and feelings the mind can't contain.

Megan had spent much of her life 're-covering' (up) the painful thoughts, feelings, and memories she hadn't known how to think about or work through on her own. I knew that learning to think together, to tolerate thinking with her mind rather than her body, to confront the isolation and secrecy that were the high-octane fuels of her eating disorder, would not be easy for her. Still, I could feel her determination to break the cycle that had dogged her for so many years and now seemed to be threatening her future. I was very glad she had reached out for connection to me. I looked forward to being part of her journey.

# hunger in the nursery

I N THE DAYS AND WEEKS that followed our first session, it became increasingly clear to Megan that food had become intertwined with the emotional relationships in her family long before she had been formally diagnosed with an eating disorder. Memories of being teased, of shame-filled trips to 'chubby' clothing departments, of sneaking food or trying to resist it, all emerged, along with painful feelings of loneliness, of having needs too much for others to handle, of there being "something wrong" with who and how she was. Not looking to cast blame, our work together was an effort at understanding the mis- and dis-connections that had occurred in her life and how they still affected her; how a 'collision of forces' between her needs and her parents' abilities to meet them had left her hungering for an elusive *'something'* to fill an emptiness that was as physical as it was emotional.

"I was thinking over the weekend about how everyone in my family always used to make fun of what a big eater I was, even as a baby," Megan looked amused as she folded her arms protectively across her torso. "I guess I was pretty fussy, too. I remember once overhearing my mother laughing with my Aunt Julia and saying, 'Remember how Megan used to drive us crazy? We used to feed her, what, thirty times a day? Just to keep her from bringing the house down!'"

Megan looked over at me, a half-smile still on her lips, waiting for my reaction. Would I laugh? Would I join the others who had entertained themselves at her expense? From what I had already learned about her history, I had a pretty good sense that Megan's lifelong hunger had been far from merely physical.

The seriousness I felt in response to her words must have been apparent. Megan shifted around on the couch and peered at me intently.

"Don't you think that's funny?" she asked.

"Not really," I replied. "Does it seem funny to you?"

Megan was surprised to learn how significant I thought her story was, how related to the development of her eating disorder. While eating disorders are often thought to begin in adolescence, my own experience with patients—along with a growing body of scientific evidence—had left little doubt in my mind about how early the seeds for their evolution are planted.

Megan was silent for several moments before continuing.

"A few months ago, my mom and I went to visit my Aunt Julia," she finally said. "I don't think I've told you about her yet. She's not really my aunt, but she and my Mom met in the hospital when her daughter Amy and I were born and our families have been close ever since. I asked them if they could tell me what Amy and I were like as babies, and they were happy to reminisce. My mom seemed to have a harder time with some of the memories than my aunt, though. I never knew that she had post-partum depression. But they both agreed that they remembered the day Amy and I were born as if it were yesterday . . ."

★   ★   ★

*"Feeding time, Mommies!"*

The night nurse cheerfully entered the semi-private hospital room and placed the pink and powdered little bundles into the arms of their mothers. Julia was thrilled with her new baby girl, the first-born to her and the proud Dad handing out cigars in the hallway. She joyously counted Amy's tiny fingers and toes over and over again; she couldn't keep her eyes off her baby's beautiful face, responding with an "ooh" or an "aah" every time Amy grimaced or changed expressions as she tried nursing.

Mary, too, held her new baby daughter in her arms, grateful that Megan didn't seem ready to nurse. Gently placing her sleeping infant at her side, she hoped to get in a few more moments of rest herself. Mary wasn't feeling terribly well. Though her active labor had lasted only a couple of hours, she was already exhausted when she arrived at the hospital. Keeping up with a two- and a four-year-old was "no picnic," she told Julia, especially at nine months pregnant! Glancing down at her newborn, Mary shuddered as she recalled her experiences nursing her two sons. Her milk never had come in properly and her nipples had been so sore and cracked, they had become infected both times. Many of her friends really seemed to enjoy nursing, but for her, it was just a nightmare.

"I *know* that nursing is best for her," Mary fretted aloud to Julia. "And I don't like to admit it, but I'm just dreading the prospect. Do you think it would be awful if I didn't even try this time?"

Julia murmured a vaguely coherent acknowledgment to her new friend. Enraptured with her own new baby, she likely had entered what psychoanalyst W. R. Bion called "reverie,"[1] her entire focus riveted on little Amy, her 'mother's intuition' already becoming informed by the slightest nuances of her baby's tiny movements and sounds. Soon, she would be able to differentiate between Amy's cries with a good deal of accuracy, feeding her when she was hungry, soothing her when her stomach was upset, rocking her when she just needed holding. Even if she didn't get it right the first time, her sensitized awareness of her baby's reactions would help her adjust her responses to Amy's needs.

Drifting off to sleep in the warm quiet room, Mary was jolted awake when Megan suddenly startled, her tiny arms and legs taut and trembling, her eyes scrunching tightly as she let out a piercing wail.

"Okay! Okay! It's okay," Mary anxiously fumbled with her gown, preparing to nurse. "Okay, baby, okay! Here goes."

Mary gingerly placed her nipple into Megan's quivering mouth. Megan latched on with an unanticipated fierceness.

"Ouch!" Mary yelped, reflexively shoving Megan away from her.

Megan startled again, her arms and legs stiffening as she emitted yet another terrified yowl.

"Oh, God," Mary began to cry. "I can't go through this again! Where is Jim, anyway? He's never here when I need him. Nurse!" she cried out into the intercom. "Could you *please* come and give her a bottle so I can get some sleep before they send me home?"

★   ★   ★

From the first moments of life, the connection between mother and infant is rooted in the feeding process. A newborn infant is put immediately to her mother's breast (or offered a bottle), the *physical* connection a metaphor for the *emotional* attachment that must also take hold if the infant is to survive and thrive. As Megan and Amy lay in their mothers' arms to nurse, the feeding provided each of them with an array of physical and emotional sensations. As Amy was held securely in her mother's arms and the warm milk began to flow, the comfort of the sucking converged with her discovery of her mother's smiling face, the sounds of her gentle cooing, the touch of her soft and soothing skin.

Amy literally and figuratively drank her mother in. Megan, too, was absorbing the emotional overtones of her first feeding. She could feel her mother's tension as she was awkwardly held, her body/mind memory recording the way her mother jumped as she began sucking at her breast. And then, suddenly, she was thrust away! No breast! No mother! Megan began to wail.

The billions of cells in Megan's and Amy's brains were already hard at work, organizing themselves into the synaptic patterns that would affect a lifetime of their eating and thinking patterns. While no single experience in and of itself determines the nature of these patterns, each experience provides a foundation for the next. Thus, even along with this first feeding, Amy's developing mind was already associating pleasure in connection with her experience of her mother. As she nursed at her own speed, starting or stopping as she willed, she was on the road to discovering that while food comforted the gnawing feeling in her stomach when she was physically hungry, a different sort of warmth enveloped her in response to her mother's soothing words and touch. As her mother carefully tracked her facial expressions, allowing her to engage or disengage as she pleased, Amy was learning from experience that she *existed* in the mind of her mother, that she had an effect on her, that her needs were worthy of response. Amy was on the road to developing a "secure attachment"[2] to her mother—a bond that was forming as she had "the repeated experience of nurturing, perceptive, sensitive, and predictable caregiving responses from her mother,"[3] which was becoming encoded in the mind/body memory system of her brain.

But what was Megan learning from her first experiences? I listened carefully for clues as she continued relaying her mother's and aunt's recollections.

★   ★   ★

By the time they left the hospital, Mary's doctors had decided that Megan was a "colicky" baby. Though she was obviously alert and engaged some of the time, she often cried or fussed and was frequently offered a feeding. But unlike Amy, who nursed eagerly, interacted briefly with her parents, and then peacefully slept, Megan seemed to both want and be resistant to the feeding. After a few moments in her mother's arms, she would turn her head from side to side, flail her arms and legs, and wail inconsolably. Julia wondered whether Megan wasn't somehow uncomfortable, whether she needed something other than a feeding.

"*I'm doing the best I can,*" Mary seethed, immediately apologizing for her "hormones." The alternative, she insisted, was walking Megan for hours, and she "*just couldn't handle that,*" especially when she thought about her impending release from the hospital and being at home alone with three children under the age of five.

When Megan and her parents arrived home from the hospital, Mary's worst fears were realized. Her two little boys had run wild with just her own mother watching them. James, age four, had refused to go to his pre-school class and was tripping two-year old Joey whenever he caught him unawares. Joey was carrying around his old ragged blanket and teddy bear and was spending most of his time sitting in the corner and sucking his thumb. Grandma was at her wit's end. Taking a few moments to fuss over the new baby, she muttered something about needing to get on the freeway before rush-hour and began packing her bags to leave.

"Mommy, Mommy, what did you bring us?" The two boys fell on their mother all at once. Overwhelmed by the cacophony, baby Megan again began to wail.

Mary collapsed into a chair. "I just don't think I can do this," she sobbed.

"Oh come on, Mary," Jim responded impatiently. "Pull yourself together. The kids need you. Can't you just give her another bottle?"

★   ★   ★

In the best of all worlds, every newborn would be welcomed into a secure and nurturing environment. But in the real world, many infants are confronted with the stress of living, even from the beginning of life. Some parents are simply not prepared to deal with the needs of a newborn. Some are affected by their own histories of strained family relations, or dealing with crises in their own lives: Work, relationships, illness, or depression. Others are overwhelmed by the unique needs of their infants—genetic, medical, constitutional—that strain their own capacities to cope. Still others, despite the best of intentions, simply cannot read their infants: There are parents who bounce when their babies need rest, who feed when the infant shows no signs of hunger, who look away when the infant searches their faces.

Naturally, it is impossible for *any* parent to be perfectly attuned to all the needs of his or her infant and child. But infants have limited capacities to excuse or to wait. Their needs are urgently experienced, their tiny bodies and minds quickly overwhelmed when those needs are misunderstood or misread. An infant may cry out because she needs holding or soothing or because something has frightened her. But if she is provided with "just another bottle" (or breast), rather than the kind of emotional nurturance she needs, she receives but half-a-meal: Her body becomes filled by the feeding, but her mind is left hungering for the emotional connection she still needs to go along with it.

★   ★   ★

"So, how did you feel when you heard your mother's and aunt's stories?" I asked Megan now.

"Oh, I don't know," she replied, shifting uncomfortably on the couch. "Part of me felt really protective of my mother. I could hear how stressed she was. But, another part just felt irritated. That really is the way she can be—so helpless and overwhelmed."

Megan's ambivalence about her mother did not surprise me. I had already been developing the sense that, while her mother was *physically* present in providing for Megan's needs, she was often intimidated by her husband and overwhelmed by the demands of her children. Mary clearly had a complex emotional history of her own, which along with the difficult circumstances of her life when Megan was born, undoubtedly limited her capacity to accurately read or respond to Megan's needs or recognize the variations in her signals. Mary felt overwhelmed, unsupported by her own mother and her husband. It wasn't her *intention* to be unavailable for Megan. She "*just couldn't handle it.*"

"That story about feeding me thirty times a day just to keep me from bringing the house down?" Megan pondered. "I guess it really isn't that funny, is it."

"No, not really," I agreed.

"You know," she said, her brow furrowed, "Amy and I are practically twin sisters. We were born on the same day and saw each other at least once a month until we went away to college. We watched the same TV shows, visited the same media sites, even had some of the same friends. But Amy never ate the way I did and never worried about her looks. And she never got an eating disorder, either."

Megan's eyes swelled with tears. "I mean, obviously Amy and I don't have the same genes or personalities," she said, reaching for a tissue. "But our parents were also *so* different from each other." Megan dabbed at her makeup and looked over at me. "It's more than just genetics, isn't it," she said.

"Nature and nurture work hand in hand," I nodded in agreement. "No matter how you and Amy came 'pre-programmed' with your own unique genetic codes, your parents' abilities to respond to you in the particular ways you needed inevitably influenced the way you each developed and how vulnerable you became to the pressures around you."

"You don't think it was because I was bottle-fed and not nursed, do you?" Megan asked, anxiously.

"It doesn't at all sound like that was the biggest issue," I replied. "It seems like your mother was having a really hard time, and it's likely that you picked up on that. I suspect you would have picked it up and reacted no matter how you were fed."

Megan nodded and gathered her things to leave. "I guess there's no gene for self-esteem, is there," she murmured.

I nodded silently in response and we slowly walked to the door.

Later that afternoon, I found myself still thinking about Megan's story. How fortunate we were to have a first-hand account of her earliest feeding experience—another piece of the puzzle of her life. Knowing how early her difficulties with food and emotional connection had begun could help us make more sense of the hungers she still struggled with in so many areas of her life—from her difficulty in being open in her relationship with Jon, to her long battle with bulimia; from her mistaken belief that her eating disorder was the result of her own "lack of willpower," "low self-esteem," or "insatiable hunger," to the shame she suffered as a result of those beliefs. Indeed, as she had suspected, her bulimia was far more than "just about food."

As I sat thinking about Megan's story, it suddenly occurred to me that it had been nearly two decades—almost to the day!—since I had first made the connection between early emotional experiences during the feeding and the later development of cyclical eating disorders. Waiting for my next patient, I closed my eyes, smiling to myself as I remembered how it had all begun with a patient I call Susie . . .

## Notes

1   Bion, W. R. (1962b). Learning from experience. In *Seven Servants: Four Works by Wilfred R. Brion.* Northvale, NJ: Jason Aronson, 1977, p. 36.
2   Bowlby, J. (1969). *Attachment and Loss, Vol. I: Attachment.* London: Hogarth Press.
3   Siegel, D. (1999). *The Developing Mind—Toward a Neurobiology of Interpersonal Experience.* New York: Guilford Press.

# *thoughts in search of a thinker*[1]

THE FIRST TIME I MET SUSIE, she described herself simply as "a bulimic," as if that was all there was to know about her. Barely five-feet tall, with long, blond hair and piercing blue eyes, twenty-eight-year-old Susie still wore pigtails and short shorts and spoke in a high-pitched childlike voice. The youngest, by a dozen years, of three sisters, Susie had been born after her mother suffered a series of miscarriages. Soon after Susie's birth, her mother returned to work in the family business, leaving Susie in the care of nannies. Susie's father, whom she adored, traveled frequently and tended to be distracted when he was at home. Susie still vividly remembered the longing and emptiness she felt each day, sitting at the front window eating candy provided by her nannies, as she waited for her mother and sisters to return. But once at home, her mother always seemed to be pre-occupied with the household and often on the phone, and her sisters had little patience for her. Even school provided her with little relief from her loneliness, sense of isolation and alienation, and shame:

"I had a *terrible* time in school," she told me. "I could never follow instructions, no matter how hard I tried. The kids all made fun of me because I was fat and stupid and unbelievably awkward. My teachers called me 'hopeless'."

Despite the family's ample resources, Susie had never been tested for learning disabilities. She was simply considered "defective," and warned by her mother never to marry or have children so as "not to pass on her genes." Susie felt that her family's primary concern was that she fit in with the country-club set in their community and not embarrass them. She still adhered to her mother's advice to "act cute" so people would be "less likely to notice" that there was "something wrong" with her.

Susie's sense of awkwardness and ineptitude—due primarily to what we later discovered to be her undiagnosed dyslexia and ADHD—culminated in what she described as a "breakdown" when she was sixteen. Not speaking and barely eating for almost a year, she was hospitalized for depression and diagnosed with anorexia. But while *not eating* had 'rules' that helped her feel organized, *eating* presented her with conflicts and choices she didn't know how to manage. How much was too much? What would happen if she broke her resolve? Forced to eat by hospital staff, it didn't take long for her to learn from other girls in the unit to purge. Once released, her early binge-eating patterns resurfaced, and unable to work or attend school, her life became organized around the solitary and isolating binge/purge rituals of bulimia.

By the time Susie began seeing me, she had moved out of her parents' home and state, hoping to "start over" and build her own life. But living alone, her terror and confusion had only intensified. She suffered from insomnia, sometimes spending the entire night bingeing, purging, and compulsively exercising. During the day her cyclical patterns continued, often causing her to be late or miss school, work, or appointments. Susie ruminated endlessly over the details of her interactions with others and spent hours on the phone with her mother and sisters, seeking their advice. Nevertheless, her difficulties in making sense of the world persisted and, along with her uncontrollable eating, filled her with shame. Despite the testing that bore out what, to me, was her obvious intelligence, Susie felt "clueless" as to how the world worked or how others "knew how to act." She was convinced that she "*just couldn't think.*"

About six months into her therapy, Susie arrived one afternoon almost twenty-minutes late for her session, looking frazzled and exhausted.

"I hardly slept at all last night," she said, stretching as she settled on the couch. "I started bingeing and purging before midnight and when I finally went to sleep, I kept waking up with the same *dreadful* nightmare I always have."

"Which nightmare is that?" I asked, not recalling Susie telling me about a recurrent dream.

"I've never really told *anyone* about it," she said, sheepishly, "at least not since I was a little girl." Susie glanced down at her clasped hands and I instantly sensed an aura of shame she associated with this dream.

"Would you like to tell me about it?" I asked, gently.

Susie nodded. "In this dream," she began softly, her voice then escalating in terror with each successive word, "I'm lying in bed and suddenly I begin to grow. I grow bigger and bigger—like a *balloon figure* in the Thanksgiving Day parade!—until I'm as big as the house and I start *oozing* out of it—through the doors, the windows, even *breaking through the ceiling!*"

Susie shivered. She reached for a throw pillow and hugged it to her chest as she continued. "When I was a child," she said, her teeth now chattering, "I would wake up from this dream almost every night *terrified*. I'd jump out of bed screaming and run around and around the house in circles until my parents would catch me and *throw* me into a bathtub filled with cold water, supposedly to calm me down. It was *horrible*. They always got so angry at me for causing such a ruckus and waking everybody up. I can still hear my mother shrieking, *'What is wrong with you, Susie!'*"

"Ever since then," she sighed, "I've stayed up at night as long as I can, trying not to fall asleep and into this dreadful dream. I eat and eat until I can't eat any more, and then . . ." She hesitated and looked away. "Then I throw up into my container, these plastic cups that I throw up into and keep stored in my closet."

Susie glanced over at me again. "I've never told anyone about this before," she said.

"I'm really glad you're telling me now," I replied softly.

Susie sighed again. "And *then*, the whole thing starts over again. I fall asleep and have the same dreadful dream all over again. I wake up so terrified I can't move. I can't breathe. *I can't even think!*"

"*I can't think.*" Susie's words riveted my attention. Suddenly it seemed as if every patient I had ever treated with an eating disorder had used this phrase at one time or another to describe their state of mind as they teetered on the brink of a binge. What did it mean to not be able to *think*, I pondered? On the surface, of course, we know that is impossible: Our minds generate thought no matter what we do. But what was the connection between Susie's sense of "not being able to think" and her persistent bouts of bingeing and purging?

As Susie lapsed into a thoughtful silence, my mind began to play on all the ways we mindlessly link thinking and eating. We say, "I can't swallow that," or "you've bitten off more than you can chew." You might want time to "digest the material," but "you can't have your cake and eat it, too." Virtually every psychoanalytic theory of development makes use of a 'digestive system model' and the early feeding relationship between mother and infant as a metaphor for how thinking begins. Did Sigmund Freud, I suddenly wondered, have any idea how closely he was describing bulimia when he said that the first decision an infant makes is whether to take food in or spit it out?[2]

Susie could think of no associations to her dream. She had no idea what brought it on or what it meant; she was simply consumed by its terror. I was deeply moved by how ashamed she appeared to be of this disturbing nightmare—as if the fact that she had it at all was evidence there really was *"something wrong"* with her.

For several days after Susie told me her dream, I couldn't get it out of my mind. I thought about the things she had talked about that day: Her struggle with food and her frustration that she "couldn't think;" her curious use of the word "dreadful" to describe her nightmare; the shame–filled revelation that she threw up into a cup she called her 'container'.

The irony of metaphor suddenly struck me. It was psychoanalyst W. R. Bion who, in his "Theory of Thinking,"[3] first introduced the term "container"[4] to describe the critical role the feeding mother plays in helping her newborn infant develop his/her innate capacity for thinking. Newborn infants, Bion asserted, cannot distinguish between their bodies and their minds. When they first experience the distress of hunger, they are unable to differentiate between the part of their discomfort that is *physical* and the part that is *emotional*. Physical and emotional are one and the same.

In the ideal course of events, a dance of sorts develops between infant and mother. The baby "projects"[5] her distress into the mother, said Bion, alerting her by crying, fussing, or other *physical* means of signaling that she is in need of feeding, attention, and care. If the mother understands the *dual physical and emotional* nature of the baby's distress, and feeds her soothing and comforting back into the baby *along with* the milk, the baby's agitated state is relieved. The terrifying feelings are 'evacuated'[6] into her mother, and mother then becomes the 'container' for the infant's distress. The baby is then able to 're-introject' (i.e., take back in) her "frightened personality in a form that she can tolerate"[7], along with the milk. As this interchange—what Bion called "normal projective identification"[8]—repeats itself again and again with each successive feeding, the baby "learns from experience"[9] that someone outside of herself—a *mother* (or other)—*exists* who understands her and can help her in times of distress. The "realization"[10] of an understanding mother, said Bion, is the equivalent of the baby's first "thought." It forms the foundation for the baby to make use of her own thoughts for abstract thinking, for restorative dreaming, and for making meaningful links with others.

However, Bion argued, if the baby is *fed*, but the mother (or other primary caregiver)—*for whatever reason*—is consistently emotionally unavailable or not responsive to her baby's needs, the baby grows increasingly agitated. Instinctively continuing to reach for relief in the feeding, she nurses with "increasing force and frequency,"[11] wailing, flailing her arms and legs, trying by every *physical* means available to her to signal her mother and achieve the critical emotional connection she needs. But if all her efforts fail, the infant is left with a terror inside—a *"nameless dread"*[12]—that disrupts her developing capacity for thinking. Her mind is flooded with chaotic and 'undigestible' "proto-thoughts"[13] that cannot be "repressed or suppressed"[14] or made unconscious. The baby becomes "hypersensitive,"[15] as she struggles with feelings she can feel, but not make sense of,[16] and thoughts that are so clouded by emotion, they cannot be used for thinking, dreaming, or making links with others. Left not only with her original toxic feelings, but the additional "negative realization"[17] of a "willfully misunderstanding"[18] mother, Bion concludes, the infant goes on to spend her life trying to find ways to 'evacuate' her distress into others, forever in search of the emotional 'container' she can never find.

As I thought about Susie's "namelessly dreadful" recurrent nightmare, a dream that so filled her with terror she "couldn't even think" (or have a different dream), Bion's theory—though intended as a theory of *thinking* disorders and not of *eating* disorders—captured my imagination. There was Susie, literally symbolizing her escalating terror with the food she ate with "increasing force and frequency"—food that grew "bigger and bigger" inside her, filling her "like a *balloon figure*," until it literally "oozed" out of her "house" (body) by way of her bulimia. There she was, frantically running in circles around her childhood home, desperately seeking a connecting emotional link that could allow the terror and chaos in her mind to be transformed into thoughts she could use for 'thinking and dreaming'. Susie's mind was so filled with 'undigestible' chaos, I realized then, that she could neither use her own thoughts for thinking when she was distressed, nor had she learned from her experiences to 'evacuate' her distress by sharing it with others. Indeed, instead of *finding* a 'container', she had become her *own* container—what I call a '**toxic container**'[19]—holding and storing her still-indistinguishable physical and emotional distress inside herself . . . until she *literally* tried to 'evacuate' it into the cup she so poignantly called her 'container'.

Susie surely had been fed as an infant—even overfed, if her belief that she had been overweight as a child was accurate. But she had never been able to achieve the kind of emotional connection she so longed for: There was always "something wrong" with Susie. Susie had spent her entire life trying to extract thought—usable, thinkable *thought*—out of the food she consumed. Now, when she insisted that she "couldn't think," I understood that her mind was being flooded, that she could not process or regulate the chaos and terror she felt, that she could neither resolve her confusion on her own, nor had she learned from her earliest experiences how to think through her emotional distress with others. Her body kept coming to the rescue, offering her a concrete, *physical* means of 'evacuating' what her mind could not contain. Susie had indeed found a makeshift physical solution for her 'undigestible' emotional problem, but it had not been a terribly effective one for her. For after every binge and purge cycle, the hunger and the longing would return, and, try as she might, the whole cycle would begin again.

★   ★   ★

Susie's dream, viewed through the lens of Bion's theory all those years before, had provided me with a powerful psychoanalytic metaphor for understanding the emotional origins of cyclical eating disorders. But would his theory and my interpretation of it hold up in light of contemporary advances in neuroscience and infant development? Could "emotional interactions that begin at the breast" indeed impact an infant's long-term development, and even lay the foundation for an eating disorder?

Well, let me tell you another story . . .

## Notes

1 This chapter was originally published as part of: Kullman, A. (2007). The 'perseverant' personality: A pre-attachment perspective on the etiology and evolution of binge/purge eating disorders. *Psychoanalytic Dialogues*, 17(5): 705–732. And previously in: Kullman, A. (1995). *The 'Autizoid' Personality and the Eating Disorder*. Unpublished Doctoral dissertation.

2 Freud, S. (1925). Negation. *Standard Edition* 19: 3–66.

3 Bion, W. R. (1962a). A theory of thinking. In *Second Thoughts: Selected Papers on Psychoanalysis*. Northvale, NJ: Jason Aronson, 1967, pp. 110–119.

4 Bion, W. R. (1962b). Learning from experience. In *Seven Servants: Four Works by Wilfred R. Bion*. Northvale, NJ: Jason Aronson, 1977, p. 90.

5 Ibid. (1962b), p. 13.

6 Ibid. (1962b), p. 13.

7 Ibid. (1962b), p. 15.

8 Bion, W. R. (1959). Attacks on linking. In *Second Thoughts: Selected Papers on Psychoanalysis*. Northvale, NJ: Jason Aronson, 1967, pp. 93–109.

9 Ibid. (1962b).

10 Ibid. (1962b), p. 113.

11 Ibid. (1962a), p. 115.

12 Ibid. (1962a), p. 116.

13 Ibid. (1962b), p. 84.

14  Ibid. (1962b), p. 8.
15  Ibid. (1962b), p. 8.
16  Ibid. (1962b), p. 18.
17  Ibid. (1962a), p. 112.
18  Ibid. (1962a), p. 117.
19  Kullman, A. (1995). The 'Autizoid' Personality and the Eating Disorder. Unpublished Doctoral dissertation. See also Kullman, A. (2007). The 'perseverant' personality: A pre-attachment perspective on the etiology and evolution of binge/purge eating disorders. *Psychoanalytic Dialogues*, 17(5): 705–732, 2007.

# missing links[1]

M IKAELA, A THIRTY-YEAR-OLD NURSERY SCHOOL TEACHER, was as excited to be pregnant with her first baby as anyone I've ever seen. Determined to be the best mother she possibly could be, Mikaela spent her entire pregnancy preparing for her newborn. She read every book on parenting and infant development she could get her hands on, and by the time little Max was born, she had an entire bookshelf filled with instruction manuals. But Max, it turned out, was not exactly what Mikaela had expected when she was expecting. He was born jaundiced—the result of liver toxins that hadn't been properly eliminated before birth. Though Max's doctors insisted that Mikaela nurse him as frequently as possible in order to help wash the toxins out of his system, Max was what the lactation nurse called a "sleepy baby." He simply wasn't interested in nursing, and particularly not at the three-hour-minimum intervals the pediatricians were insisting upon. When Mikaela brought Max into a session when he was three-days old, she was beside herself. Max was resisting the feeding, thrusting his head from side to side, spitting up, fussing as she tried to get him to latch on, and promptly falling asleep even when he did. A battle royal was in the making. Mikaela wanted to do what was right, what the pediatricians had told her would be best for her baby, but her baby clearly had not gotten the memo!

As I watched the two of them struggle, I found myself concerned about how easily a situation like this could set the stage for an eating disorder—for future battles over food or for food becoming an area of conflict for little Max. While far more is known today about pre-natal influences than in Bion's time, research has shown that emotional interactions that begin with the earliest feedings do indeed influence the foundations of thinking, literally impacting the architecture of what neuropsychologist Allan Schore calls the "experience-dependent" right (emotional) hemisphere of the brain.[2]

"The brain gobbles up its external environment in bits and chunks through its sensory system," wrote researcher Ronald Kotulak. "Then the digested world is reassembled in the form of trillions of connections between brain cells that are constantly growing or dying, or becoming stronger or weaker, depending on the richness of the banquet."[3]

As Mikaela held little Max during the feeding—at the exact ten-inch distance at which infants see best[4]—her more developed and differentiated nervous system was interacting with Max's newly-developing regulatory systems in order to create the "mutual regulation of [their] vital endocrine, autonomic, and central nervous systems."[5] Mikaela's ability to be sensitive in registering and responding to Max's moment-to-moment state changes and rhythms would influence his ability to process and regulate his emotions and their intensities,[6] and to form what Schore called "coherent responses to cope with stressors."[7] Her ability to engage with Max in "interactive repair"[8] when there were inevitable disruptions in their connection would facilitate Max's ability to regulate his own emotional states.[9]

These early experiences—especially during the critical first two months of Max's life while his brain was initially organizing—would "frame [Max's] subsequent transactions with the environment"[10] and lay the foundation for a secure or insecure attachment. "Attachment relationships," reflected neuropsychologist Daniel Siegel:

> Are crucial in organizing not only ongoing experience, but the neuronal growth of the developing brain . . . [They] have a direct effect on the domains of mental functioning . . . [and] may serve to create the central foundation from which the mind develops.[11]

Mikaela's understanding of Max's mind would "facilitate [Max's] . . . general understanding of minds"—what Fonagy et al. called "reflective function"[12]—and his self-organization through the mediation of secure attachment.

Through the intimacy of the feeding, Mikaela and Max's minds thus needed to work together to bring Max into the world of thought and relatedness to himself and others, with it being Mikaela's role to *invite* Max into the interpersonal world by way of her emotional interactions with him. This form of what I call '**mutual re-*cognition***'—a conjoint sharing of emotional connection and cognition (or thought)[13]—would form the basis for Max's newly-developing capacity to make sense of his existence in the world. It would lay the foundation for self-regulation—that internal state of equilibrium or homeostasis—that would enable him to focus on subsequent stages of his development.

But what could happen if Mikaela *wasn't* able to be accurately attuned to Max's unique needs? What if she remained frightened or preoccupied with her own thoughts or distress during or surrounding the feeding and unable to accurately read or predictably respond to Max's signals? Such unpredictability could lead to alternating states of hyper-(or hypo-) arousal in Max, as his needs might be inconsistently gratified or misread.[14] Research has shown that parents who have abrupt shifts in their states of mind, who give conflicting, confusing, or fear-inducing messages to their infants, and/or who do not initiate *repair* of broken or disrupted connections, may indeed induce what Bion called *"nameless dread"*—or what Perry et al. called fear and/or terror states—in their infants.[15] This could lay the foundation for an insecure (ambivalent, disorganized, or disoriented) attachment to their mothers.[16]

Infants are acutely sensitive to the emotional states of their mothers. Research has shown that when a mother exhibits unresolved fear, her baby can sense the emotion as early as forty-two minutes after birth.[17] In one of the earliest infant development studies, Ainsworth and Bell found that infants were so sensitive to their mother's emotional states, they were impacted by her *motives* during the feeding, even if those motives were benign: Babies who were routinely nursed for any reason other than the gratification of their needs—whose mothers, for example, tried to distract them or get them to sleep longer—showed signs of insecure attachment by twelve months of age.[18] Nor does it require abuse or maltreatment to induce such a terror state in the newly-developing brain of an infant: Researchers Hesse and Main described "a second generation effect of more subtle behaviors resulting from the parent's own frightened or frightening ideation surrounding [their own] experiences of trauma."[19] That is, "mental and emotional difficulties may later arise in offspring whose parents are in no way directly maltreating and may even in some cases ordinarily be sensitive to infant signals and communications."[20]

In fact, it doesn't take much to *permanently* install such a fear-state in the implicit or unremembered memory system of a living being. Sometimes a *single* fear stimulus is sufficient to lay the foundation for a lifetime of fearful responses. Neuroscientist Joseph LeDoux identified a very early-developing "pre-cognitive"[21] fearful state—what he calls *"emotional perseveration"*[22]— that results in the same fearful response repeating itself over and over again. Unlike the *cognitive* perseveration seen in dissociative or obsessive-compulsive disorders that is generated in the para-sympathetic nervous system and later-developing areas of the brain, emotional perseveration is generated in the *sympathetic* (excitatory) nervous system, which is already 'online' and fully-functional at birth. Once established, says LeDoux, emotional perseveration is "exceedingly difficult to extinguish,"[23] and is so tenacious that it can "impair a baby's decision-making ability in emotional situations"[24] for a lifetime. In the face of future re-activated fear-inducing situations, he concludes, the 'thinking' brain (cortex) shuts down, the fear and threat-assessing center (amygdala) instantly reacts, and "because they cannot properly regulate fear circuits, these individuals continually experience fear and anxiety *[even] in . . . safe situations*"[25] [italics added].

Could it be, I began to wonder, that the cyclical eating disorders that are often thought to begin in adolescence and/or be responses to abuse, neglect, separation conflicts, or peer and cultural pressures, actually *begin* as early, fear-based responses to a frightened, frightening, or unpredictable parent or primary caregiver? Could it be that the same instinctual circuitry that triggers survival-based food-seeking behaviors in the newborn, but remains unmediated by emotional attunement and containment, fails to be extinguished? Over-whelming emotional experiences might then repeatedly trigger these same synaptic patterns, and the infant—becoming the child, adolescent, and adult—might continue reaching for connection in the original way—via the feeding.[26] Since we know that "neurons that fire together, wire together"[27] and "states become traits,"[28] scientific evidence seemed to be pointing toward confirmation of what by then had become my working hypothesis:

> When misattunement occurs simultaneously with the instinctual process of food-seeking, reaching for emotional connection by way of the feeding remains encoded in implicit memory as the (limbic system's) automatic "go to" solution in the face of overwhelming emotional experience.[29]

Now sitting with Mikaela in the warmth of my consulting room, watching the strain and tension on her face and in her body as she struggled to get Max to nurse, I was keenly aware of how terrified she was that she would somehow cause lasting harm to her precious newborn. I knew she was aware that difficulties surrounding the feeding often provide the earliest clues to distress in an infant, with signs of budding anxiety, depression, and fearfulness already identifiable in babies just a few hours, days, or weeks old. In the absence of diagnosed medical conditions, babies who are colicky, children who resist feeding, excessively spit up their food, suffer with frequent stomach upsets, or become obese may already be struggling to manage 'undigestible' emotional distress they cannot otherwise contain on their own.

So, what could happen if Mikaela continued to struggle with Max to try and get him to nurse? What if she insisted on "doing it right" despite all his signals? With all her good intentions, I could imagine the spiraling effect such an early fearful experience surrounding the feeding (if left unrepaired) could have on Max's subsequent development: If the critical emotional connection to his mother failed, a secure attachment to her could be compromised. If his attachment was insecure (ambivalent, disorganized, or disoriented), he could have difficulty separating and individuating into his own unique self. Without the ability to think together with his mother, Max's ability to understand his own mind and the minds of others, as well as his ability to transform emotions into symbolic thinking by finding words for his feelings, could be derailed. Max could have difficulty learning from experience to "make use of an object"[30] who was emotionally unavailable to him, or develop "the capacity to be alone"[31]—i.e., to self-regulate—in the absence of an attuned mother. While children are normally physically contained by the adults in their environment—told what to do, and how and when to do it—by the time Max reached adolescence and would be expected to reason with increasing clarity and function with increasing autonomy, his difficulties in thinking through his emotional experiences on his own could become overwhelming. It is at this point, in fact, that many eating disorders are first—or finally—diagnosed.[32]

How could I both reassure Mikaela and help her navigate her dilemma?

"What would happen," I asked Mikaela gently, "if you just once tried letting Max sleep for as long as he wants? He's going to get hungry," I reasoned. "What if you gave him the opportunity to come to the feeding on his own?"

Mikaela was hesitant—as was I—to disregard her pediatricians' instructions. Nevertheless, we agreed that it was worth a try. We decided to set a five-hour 'max'imum beyond which she would awaken Max for a feeding.

Several days later, Mikaela brought Max back with her to her session. Despite the sleepless nights she was now experiencing, her face was aglow, and she and Max looked as peacefully engaged with one another as they possibly could be.

"It *was* almost five hours the first time," she told me. "I was really getting worried. But then, it was four-and-a-half, and then four, and then three. Now he's alert, his bilirubin (a measure of the toxins) is normal, and he's nursing with no problem!"

Crisis averted! Though they'd had a difficult beginning, Mikaela and her baby were able to work things out with one another. When Mikaela was able to follow Max's cues and allow him to set the pace of his feeding (within reasonably safe limits), her attunement and understanding of his needs were communicated to Max and the challenging situation was repaired. Max was back on the road to forming a secure attachment to his mother, and Mikaela was on the road to becoming the containing mother to Max she so longed to be.

As I integrated Bion's "Theory of Thinking" with developmental research and my own clinical experience in this way, cyclical eating disorders began to make more and more sense to me. Just as the newborn infant returns again and again to the breast or bottle, with mental capacities capable only of concluding that it is the *feeding* that brings about emotional relief, so I came to believe that people with cyclical eating disorders return again and again to the food, to the 'elemental' milk, that still holds out the promise of relief. What begins as *persistence* and *perseverance* in the effort at finding an emotional '*thinking*' connection to the mother by way of the feeding becomes *perseveration*—an inability to interrupt this early, instinctual pattern, even though the longed-for emotional connection can no longer be found in this way. A lifelong yearning is thus set in motion, an insatiable psychic and somatic hunger, impacting all subsequent stages of development and laying the foundation for what I call the perseverant personality.[33]

## Notes

1  Some material in this chapter was originally published in: Kullman, A. (2007). The 'perseverant' personality: A pre-attachment perspective on the etiology and evolution of binge/purge eating disorders. *Psychoanalytic Dialogues*, 17(5): 705–732. And previously in: Kullman, A. (1995). *The 'Autizoid' Personality and the Eating Disorder*. Unpublished doctoral dissertation.

2  Schore, A. N. (1994). *Affect Regulation and the Origin of the Self: The Neurobiology of Emotional Development*. Hillsdale, NJ: Lawrence Erlbaum, p. 7.

3  Kotulak, R. (1996). *Inside the Brain: Revolutionary Discoveries of How the Mind Works*. Kansas City, MO: Andrews McMeel, p. 4.

4  Stern, D. (1985). *The Interpersonal World of the Infant*. New York: Basic Books,

5 Hofer, M. A. (1990). Early symbiotic processes: Hard evidence from a soft place. In A. Glick & S. Bone (eds), *Pleasure Beyond the Pleasure Principle*. New Haven, CT: Yale University Press, p. 71.

6 Stern, D. (1983). The early differentiation of self and other. In S. Kaplan & J.D. Lichtenberg (eds), *Reflections on Self-Psychology*. Hillsdale, NJ: Analytic Press.

7 Schore, A. (2001). Effects of a secure attachment relationship on right brain development, affect regulation, and infant mental health. *Infant Mental Health Journal*, 22(1–2): 7–66.

8 Tronick, E. Z. (1989). Emotions and emotional communication in infants. *Psychologist*, 44: 112–119, p. 112.

9 Beebe, B. & Lachmann, F. (1994). Representations and internalization in infancy: Three principles of salience. *Psychoanalytic Psychology*, 11: 127–165.

10 Sroufe, L. A., Carlson, E. A., Levy, A. K., & Egeland, B. (1999). Implications of attachment theory for developmental psychopathology. *Development & Psychopathology*, 11: 1–13, p. 5.

11 Siegel, D. (1999). *The Developing Mind: Toward a Neurobiology of Interpersonal Experience*. New York: Guilford Press, p. 68.

12 Fonagy, P., Target, M., & Gergely, G., (2000). Attachment and borderline personality disorder: A theory and some evidence. *Psychiatric Clinics of North America*. 23(1): 103–122.

13 Kullman, A. (1995). *The 'Autizoid' Personality and the Eating Disorder*. Unpublished doctoral dissertation.

14 Main, M. (2000). The organized categories of infant, child, and adult attachment: Flexible vs. inflexible attention under attachment-related stress. *Journal of the American Psychoanalytic Association*, 48(4): 1055–1096.

15 Perry, B. D., Pollard, R. A., Blakely, T. L, Baker, W. L., & Vigilante, D. (1995). Childhood trauma, the neurobiology of adaptation, and 'use-dependent' development of the brain: How states become traits. *Infant Mental Health Journal*, 16: 271–291.

16 Hesse, E. & Main, M. (2000). Disorganized infant, child, and adult attachment: Collapse in behavioral and attentional strategies. *Journal of the American Psychoanalytic Association*, 48(4): 1099–1127.

17 Decety, J. & Meltzoff, A. N. (2011). Empathy, imitation, and the social brain. In A. Copland & P. Goldie (eds), *Empathy: Philosophical and Psychological Perspectives*. New York: Oxford University Press, pp. 58–81.

18 Ainsworth, M. & Bell, S. (1969). Some contemporary patterns of mother–infant interaction in the feeding situation. In A. Ambrose (ed.), *Stimulation in early infancy*. New York: Academic Press, 1969, pp. 133–170.

19 Hesse, E. & Main, M., (2000), p. 1103.

20 Ibid. (2000), p. 1117.

21 LeDoux, J. (1996). *The Emotional Brain: The Mysterious Underpinnings of Emotional Life*. New York: Simon and Schuster, p. 249.

22 Ibid. (1996), p. 249

23 Ibid. (2002). *Synaptic Self: How Our Brains Become Who We Are*. New York: Viking, p. 217.

24 Ibid. (2002), p. 217.

25 Ibid. (2002), p. 217.

26  Kullman, A. (2007). The 'perseverant' personality: A pre-attachment perspective on the etiology and evolution of binge/purge eating disorders. *Psychoanalytic Dialogues*, 17(5): 705–732.

27  Hebb, D. O. (1949). The Organization of Behavior: A Neuropsychological Theory. In Siegel D. (1999). *The Developing Mind: Toward a Neurobiology of Interpersonal Experience*. New York: Jason Aronson, p. 26.

28  Perry, B. D., Pollard, R. A., Blakely, T. L., Baker, W. L., & Vigilante, D. (1995). Childhood trauma, the neurobiology of adaptation, and 'use-dependent' development of the brain: How states become traits. *Infant Mental Health Journal*, 16: 271–291.

29  Kullman, A. (2007). The 'perseverant' personality: A pre-attachment perspective on the etiology and evolution of binge/purge eating disorders. *Psychoanalytic Dialogues*, 17(5): 705–732.

30  Winnicott, D. W. (1968). The use of an object and relating through identifications. In *Playing and Reality*. London: Tavistock, 1971, pp. 86–94.

31  Ibid. (1958). The capacity to be alone. *International Journal of Psychoanalysis*, 39: 416–420.

32  Kullman, A. (2007).

33  Kullman, A. (2007).

# Part two

# 'Thinking' with the body

## The perseverant personality

five

# *mind on a merry-go-round*[1]

"I'VE BEEN TRYING TO FIGURE OUT why I automatically go to eating," Susie began her session, barely able to contain herself. She had arrived uncharacteristically early for her appointment, eager to tell me what she had been thinking about over the weekend. "I think I punish myself part of the time for not being able to do what I'm trying to do," she continued breathlessly, "and the rest of the time I push myself harder and harder, constantly trying to get ahead so maybe then I won't panic as much. This sense of *panic* comes over me when I'm not sure how something will come out. Then I have a fear of trying, because I might not make it. *Then* I worry: Am I going to feel worse if I don't make it, or if I don't even try? But if I get scared along the way and *eat*, do I *ever* get to know the result? And then, if I *do* accomplish something, I'm not sure if I can feel good about it and claim it, or whether I should start worrying about something else that I haven't done yet."

Susie took a deep breath and audibly exhaled as she slumped back against the sofa cushions.

"It's like I keep trying to show that I'm worthy," she sighed, her exuberance fading, "but I can't ever get there. Nothing ever feels simple to me. I don't know how to deal with good feelings any more than bad ones. I'm known in my family for how 'flexible' I am, but that's because I'm so confused on the inside. That 'flexibility' is really my *chaos*."

Susie's mind was on a merry-go-round, I found myself thinking, the same chaotic thoughts and feelings churning around and around in her head. Though she was highly intelligent and perceptive, she constantly questioned her own abilities and lived in fear of making a mistake. She was excruciatingly sensitive to the input of others, never quite knowing what to take in and what not to take in, what came from the inside of her and what from the outside. At times, she would turn an interchange over and over in her mind, micro-analyzing every nuance, alert to any clue she was being rejected or misunderstood. And weaving their way in and around it all were the 'food thoughts' that invariably took over her mind, replacing all her other thinking and compelling her to eat.

Like an intricately-woven tapestry, Susie's cyclical eating and thinking patterns wove the fabric of the perseverant personality—what I define as:

> A solitary and circular mode of being, thinking, and relating that is organized around a sustained physical and emotional reliance on the feeding as a means of thought processing and emotional regulation.[2]

In essence, Susie had learned to 'think' with her body; her body and mind worked *interchangeably*, rather than *interactively*. Overwhelming emotional experiences persistently triggered involuntary physical responses—'food thoughts', cravings, urges to starve or purge, faulty body images—rather than the thought-based and inter-personal solutions she needed to help soothe and regulate her emotional states. In its most literal sense, Susie (and others with perseverant personalities) had learned to use *food for thought*.

The ideas for the perseverant personality evolved out of my work and research with eating-disordered patients like Susie, Megan, and others, who presented with a uniquely intertwined body/mind personality organization, unlike any I could find in the DSM (Diagnostic and Statistical Manual of the American Psychological Association)[3] or in psychoanalytic literature. These patients, who all suffered with some form of a cyclical eating disorder, shared a *solitary and circular* mode of thought processing and an apparent confusion between that which is processed by the body and that by the mind. Unlike my 'restrictor' patients, who struggled with anorexia, chronic starvation dieting, or chronic (non-medically induced) obesity, and whose lives were organized around keeping food (and/or potentially toxic emotions) *out* of themselves, the patients I came to think of as 'perseverant' longed to *take in*. And unlike individuals who had *withdrawn* from emotional connection in response to traumatic inter-actions with their parents or others, the individuals I came to see as perseverant had neither *found* their emotional "thinking" (m)others to begin with, nor had they given up their attempts to find her. Their lives were organized around an endless, repetitive, and ultimately fruitless search, using their *bodies* to reach out for the emotional connections that constantly eluded them.

While cyclical eating disorders have been diagnosed across the spectrum of psychological disorders, none of the traditional classifications seem to capture the uniquely-intertwined thinking and eating patterns of individuals who suffer them. Diagnoses of 'borderline' or 'narcissistic' personality organizations, for example, can be applied to *some* patients with binge/purge eating dis-orders, but not to all, and not all of the time. Classifications such as 'obsessive compulsive' or 'dissociative' disorders include *some* characteristics seen in binge/purge eating disorders, but fail to account for their intertwined body/mind nature—nor do they necessarily include dysfunctional relationships with food. On the other hand, DSM categories for eating disorders tend to focus on the *physical* aspects and enactments of these disorders, often looking to medical models or methods used to achieve a particular body size or weight, rather than to consistent psychodynamic criteria.[4] And even further confounding accurate diagnoses, many research studies do not differentiate between what I call '**restrictor disorders**' (e.g., anorexia) and cyclical (perseverant) binge/purge disorders (e.g., bulimia)—which, as we shall see, have significant emotional and developmental differences between them.

The perseverant personality, as I conceive of it, is literally embodied *in and by* the body/mind enactments of cyclical binge/purge eating disorders. Because these thinking and eating patterns are so uncannily similar in individuals who suffer these disorders, I believe they reflect a near–ubiquitous, fear-based response to failures in emotional connection beginning with the earliest feedings of life that have set the stage for predictable perseverative and physical responses to emotional distress. And because these patterns harken back to this earliest, pre-attachment stage of development, I also suggest that the perseverant personality pre-dates, creates vulnerability for, and can eventually co-exist with other, later-developing, psychological conditions. The infant who begins life hungering for emotional connection is more likely to become vulnerable to experiences of shame, trauma, abuse, and so forth, as he or she develops. Such secondary trauma or abuse might then elicit an *overlay* of psychopathology *in addition* to the "emotional perseveration" established early-on that becomes organized around food. This 'layering' may shed light on why cyclical eating disorders are so frequently seen across the diagnostic spectrum and are so frequently misdiagnosed.

Because food and thought remain so inextricably linked in the psyches of people with perseverant personalities, a cyclical eating disorder in some form is invariably a key element of their personalities. But people with perseverant personalities share far more than their eating patterns. They also share what I believe to be consistent and predictable thought patterns, belief systems, fears, self-talk, and/or emotional enactments that are as intricately interwoven with each other as they are with the physical enactments of their eating disorders. These characteristic patterns, which manifest *simultaneously* rather than *sequentially*, include:

- An enmeshed body and mind that work interchangeably rather than interactively
- A solitary and circular mode of thought processing
- A conscious and chaotic sense of disorganization
- Fear and dread
- Shame and an intransigent belief in their own "toxic" natures
- Hypersensitivity and an absence of effective defense mechanisms
- Impaired decision-making
- Emotionally-based language or communication difficulties
- Rhythmic and repetitive physical enactments mirroring their emotional perseveration
- Challenges in relationships to self and others
- The ongoing and literal use of food for thought.

A perseverant personality is thus steeped in what I call a solitary and circular **'one-person psychology'**, where thinking alone rather than together with others is the primary mode of thought-processing, where food serves as one's most reliable and trusted companion, and where secrecy and shame conspire to create the notorious "low self-esteem" and negative body images traditionally associated with eating disorders. For the individual with a perseverant personality, fear lurks just beneath the surface, words for feelings are often absent or cannot be described, tolerated, or experienced, and self-regulation is an ongoing challenge.

In each of the following chapters in Part Two, *'Thinking' with the body*, I highlight these characteristic elements of the perseverant personality individually, while at the same time demonstrating their inevitable interplay. Taken together, I hope to illustrate how uncontained emotional states routinely interrupt the daily lives and ordinary thinking of intelligent, creative people with perseverant personalities, leaving them vulnerable to 'falling through the cracks' and into their often hidden and shame-ridden eating disorders. As we shall see, the short circuit occurs at the intersection of thinking and feeling.

## Notes

1 Some material in this chapter was originally published in: Kullman, A. (1995). *The 'Autizoid' Personality and the Eating Disorder.* Unpublished Doctoral dissertation. See also: Kullman, A. (2007). The 'perseverant' personality: A pre-attachment perspective on the etiology and evolution of binge/purge eating disorders. *Psychoanalytic Dialogues,* 17(5): 705–732, 718.
2 Kullman, A. (2007), p. 718.
3 American Psychaitric Association (2000). *Diagnostic and Statistical Manual of Mental Disorders* (4th edn). Washington, DC.
4 American Psychiatric Association (2000; 2013). Diagnostic and Statistical Manual of Mental Disorders (4th and 5th edns). Washington, DC.

# *thinking alone*

I HEARD AMANDA ENTER the waiting room ten minutes before her session was scheduled to begin. I opened the door to find her pacing, hair disheveled, eyes wide with fear. She brushed past me and headed into the consulting room.

"My oral defense is *tomorrow*," she whispered hoarsely, continuing to pace in front of the couch. "I tried to get it delayed, but I couldn't. I called in sick today, but I don't know what I'm going to do. I'm not ready! I keep writing the same sentence over and over again. *What am I going to do?*"

Amanda collapsed onto the sofa and drew her knees up to her chest. She covered herself with the throw blanket and huddled in the corner, her terror permeating the room.

"I can't stop bingeing and purging," she said, reaching for a tissue and rubbing her eyes. "I know it's not the food. I'm not even hungry. I'm just so scared. I don't know what I'm going to do. *I'm so scared.*"

"What's the 'scared'?" I asked her, quietly. "Tell me about the 'scared'."

As I waited for Amanda to respond, my mind was revisited by Bion's metaphor: If during the feeding, a baby's 'frightened personality' is not 'fed back' to her in a form that she can tolerate, she is left with a terror inside— a "*nameless dread*"—that disrupts her capacity for thinking. Sitting with Amanda now, her dread felt alive in the room. I had seen her in variations of this state of terror numerous times in the months we had been working together. We had grappled again and again with the sense of fear and foreboding she had lived with for as long as she could remember—the fear and dread she had always tried to feed with food.

When Amanda first came to see me, she felt like her life was spinning out of control. She had begun the academic year feeling good about her doctoral research project and the classes she was assigned as a Teaching Assistant in the Mathematics Department at the university. But the pressures of preparing lectures, grading papers, holding office hours, and completing her thesis had left her feeling overwhelmed and fearful. Amanda had grown increasingly isolated, rarely socializing with classmates, often spending days on end holed-up in her tiny campus apartment with the drapes drawn. Her attempts at "pulling herself together" by "eating healthy" and running twice a day more often than not disintegrated into marathons of bingeing and purging. Amanda felt sick to her stomach much of the time, unable to keep up and unable to keep anything down.

As we explored her history, I learned that Amanda was the only child of parents who had arrived in this country with little more than the proverbial shirts on their backs. While her father had managed to integrate into their new environs, her mother had never acclimated and still barely spoke the language. Amanda had spent her life trying to reach her introverted and depressed mother. She had heard a few stories from her father about her mother's traumatic experiences in, and escape from, their war-torn native country, but never once had she heard her mother talk about her past—or the family she had left behind and lost. Amanda's heart ached for her mother. She remembered even as a small child trying her hardest to bring a smile to her mother's face, but nothing she ever did seemed to make a difference. Amanda still recalled the fantasy that had sustained her throughout her childhood whenever she was required to leave her mother's side: She would imagine that there was a string fastened to her waistband, attached to her mother at the other end. She would spend the entire day keeping track of the imaginary string, making sure it did not become unfastened or entangled —a rich and moving metaphor for me of her otherwise untethered existence.

Amanda's father, himself a reticent man, had tried his best to make up for her mother's emotional absence. But bound as he was to the culture in which he had been raised, he had a hard time breaking through formality to relate to his only child. Amanda was expected to spend her time building her academic resume and was rarely granted permission to socialize with friends or engage in what her father considered to be frivolous activities. Amanda managed to forge a link with her father around their mutual love of math, often begging him to challenge her with equations, reveling in the moments she merited his reserved acknowledgment or praise. But as the emotional equations in her life grew more complex, her isolation and fearfulness only compounded. Amanda carried a heavy burden of guilt and responsibility, a sense that she wasn't enough, that nothing she ever did could make up for her mother's losses or brighten her father's life. She couldn't recall when her bingeing and purging first began, she told me. She couldn't remember *not* throwing up.

Amanda had neither been overtly abused nor neglected as a child, but in the absence of her parents' emotional attunement, she had grown up without the joyous "mirroring"[1] every child needs. She had missed out on the discovery that she 'existed' in the hearts and minds of others, or that she had an impact on them. She had not learned from her experiences that her thoughts, feelings, or sensations were similar in kind or in nature, or at least *comprehensible*, to others. Amanda's thinking had developed in a solitary and circular fashion—an '**autizoid**'[2] or 'one-person psychology',[3] as I call it— informed primarily by her own terror-filled perceptions and the unfiltered and unfathomable elements she took in. There had been no nourishing 'meeting of the minds'[4] to soothe her senses or help her learn to think together with others as a means of regulating her emotional states. As she struggled to understand how other peoples' minds work—what Fonagy and Target (1997) call "reflective function"[5]—her own mind remained colored by chaos: What to take in and what not to take in? What came from the inside of her, and what from the outside? The thoughts and feelings she had tried to project into her parents in the hope of having them contained and made 'digestible' for her had essentially been 'returned to sender', her own—and *their*—psychic addresses remaining unknown.

Amanda had succeeded in becoming 'perfectly' competent in other areas of her life. From "straight A's" in school to running marathons, the same persistence that had characterized her attempts at reaching her parents manifested in her drive to be the best at anything she attempted. But lacking the experience of thinking through her thoughts and feelings together with her parents, her internal world was fraught with chaos. She was acutely sensitive to interactions, worrying what others *really* thought or meant, wondering whether she was missing out on subtle references or colloquialisms everyone else seemed to understand. She felt ashamed of things she didn't know, things she thought she *ought to* know, things she imagined came easily to others but not to her. She dampened her own creativity by worrying that her efforts were not good enough. While her 'left-brain' intellectual capacities had developed in accordance with her genetic endowment, her fearfulness and perseveration made it difficult for her to make sense of her own perceptions or make full use of the cognitive capacities with which she was so richly endowed. Left to process her fears, confusion, conflict, distress, even her *joys* on her own, Amanda was frequently thrown back on her own limited psychic resources for survival. Whenever thoughts she could not 'think', or process on her own threatened to engulf her, the instinctual drive to survive by way of the feeding was re-awakened. Whenever chaos threatened to overwhelm her, she was hurled back to a time when, as Bion had put it, "the breast was indistinguishable from an idea in the mind."[6]

Each time Amanda was catapulted into a binge/terror state, we had carefully followed its footprint and arrived at the doorstep of fear. We had combed through the helplessness and terror of the baby and child she once was, the child who had hungered for soothing and comforting, but had needed to settle for 'half a meal'. Amanda's fear had overshadowed her life. It lurked just beneath the surface, coloring her decisions, her actions, her thoughts about herself and others, even as she went about the everyday motions of her life. Fear wears a cloak of many colors. Amanda was afraid she wasn't good enough, that she would be disappointed or disappointing, that she would make mistakes, that others wouldn't "get" her, that she would be "outed," seen wanting, a fraud. She was afraid to be hurt, wounded, shattered, humiliated, abandoned. She had spent *forever* trying to figure things out on her own, living a secret inner life, afraid to bare herself to others, afraid of what she couldn't *bear* or allow herself to feel.

Eating took the edge off it, but not really. It only distracted her, putting her out of her misery only for as long as it took to tell herself that she'd feel better if she had whatever it was she imagined in the moment she couldn't live without. Amanda longed to be filled with what she needed, even though she didn't know what that was. There was a hunger, a longing; she could feel it in her mouth, her throat, her gut. She *needed*. But what was it she needed? She didn't know. She had tried to feed the emptiness, the longing, the terror with food, hoping that that perfect chocolate mousse cake would somehow fill the hole. But it didn't. It only coated the hole, encasing it in a protective layer, shielding her for a few moments from experiencing the excruciating burning pain of the terror, of the unknown *something* she longed for but could never find.

But the saddest irony of all, as Amanda was beginning to recognize, was that in the end, eating didn't really work. The more she turned to food to try and help herself, the more fragile and dependent she felt, the more terrified she became. In the moment, food felt like her only option. And, for the infant she once had been, food had indeed meant that help was on its way. But for the person she now was, the 'promise' of food was the *real* fraud; it was a taunting temptress, a ruse. It came for a moment, seduced her with promises, but then left her alone; full, but empty. She was left with the fear.

Now, that fear lived on. Amanda binged and purged to keep herself calm, to not to rock the boat, to try and be what she thought others wanted her to be. She ate so she had something to hold on to, so that her inner self would not be hurled, untethered, into the universe. She binged and purged for a myriad of reasons, each one of which was rooted in fear.

"Can you tell me about the fear?" I urged her again, gently.

"I keep seeing all those eyes staring at me," she replied. "What will they be thinking? What if I just freeze and can't think of what to say? What if my voice shakes? What if I can't remember the equations or the statistics—or even my own name?" Amanda's voice escalated with each terrifying possibility.

I listened intently for the context of her experience. How could we break it down into 'digestible' components, into thoughts her 'frightened personality' could tolerate and re-integrate back into herself?

"Who is going to be at the defense?" I asked.

"My committee," she replied, "And the head of my department. Maybe some people in the gallery."

"Anyone you expect will be hostile or critical?"

Amanda thought for a moment. "No," she replied, tentatively. "I don't think so. They've all been so supportive of me. It's just that I can't think very well on my feet—especially when I'm anxious. What if they ask me something I haven't thought about? Or if they find a hole in my formulations that I can't defend?"

"Well," I said, thinking for a moment, "it seems to me that any time you've talked about your work, or I've asked you about your research or conclusions, you've been crystal clear—knowledgeable, confident, and able to explain your arguments."

"Yes, but what if someone asks me something I can't think of an answer to?"

"Hmm," I considered. "I guess you could always say that that's an interesting question and you'll have to think about it and get back to them. Or you could ask them if *they* have any particular thoughts about it. Or you could even say that maybe you or someone else might think about doing some post-doc research on the subject in the future!"

Amanda's face broke into a broad smile and she laughed out loud. "Oh!" she exclaimed. "I didn't think of any of that! Yes, I could say those things!

And . . . and maybe I could even ask my advisor to ask a question or jump in if she sees my mind going blank!"

"There you go!" I replied, mirroring her enthusiasm. "That's a great idea!"

Amanda sat up straight on the couch, her body now animated, her demeanor transformed.

"I just get so afraid," she said. "I can't even think or speak. I don't know *what* to do with myself when I get into that state. I feel frozen; it's like a panic-attack on steroids. Eating feels like the only thing that keeps me from going crazy, but then after I eat, I feel ten times worse."

Amanda took a deep breath and readied herself to leave.

"I feel *so* much better now," she said, her face transformed. "I feel like I'm going to be okay."

I smiled as we walked to the door together. How relatively little it had taken to re-assure her, to let Amanda know that she wasn't alone, that she didn't need to come up with all the answers on her own, that others existed who could help her *think* in times of distress.

Amanda's longing for emotional connection that had begun in infancy was a longing for *mind*, for the ability to think clearly, to function in the face of overwhelming anxiety. Food staved off the chaos. It held the promise of reassurance, of safety, of not being alone anymore. Amanda's eating disorder was no less than a measure of terror. As we were slowly sorting out the psychic from the somatic, the concrete from the abstract, Amanda's capacity to *think*, to process and tolerate her own emotional experiences was developing and strengthening. Together we had taken another small step toward helping her transform her fear into manageable emotion and her chaos into thoughts she could use for thinking. Her hunger for connection was beginning to be fed.

## Notes

1   Winnicott, D. W. (1971). Mirror-role of Mother and Family in Child Development. In *Playing and Reality*. London: Tavistock, pp. 111–118.
2   Kullman, A. (1995) *The 'Autizoid' Personality and the Eating Disorder*. Unpublished doctoral dissertation.

Note: Amanda's singular and solitary—or what I call '*autizoid*'—mode of thought processing was so pronounced in her and my other patients with cyclical eating disorders that I initially viewed it as the primary element or characteristic of what later became the "perseverant personality." Writing of "The 'autizoid' personality and the eating disorder," I described what appeared to me to be a solitary, life-long search for the "object-(m)other" in the feeding that begins '*on the road*' to object-relatedness (pre-attachment), and impacts every subsequent stage of a child's development:

> The 'autizoid' *longs for* the psychic connection to the (m)other she can never find. For reasons unknown and incomprehensible to her, her (m)other cannot allow a psychical connection to occur. It is not that her (m)other is not '*there*'. The infant, through her other developing senses, finds the *concrete, physical* (m)other. She watches her and imitates her actions; she hears her words, breathes her in, tastes her milk. She learns from the *concrete* experiences before her . . . What is denied this infant are the *abstract* qualities of relatedness, the (m)other as an empathic, receptive container. The link that under normal conditions comes through *thinking together* with her (m)other does not exist for this infant. Her affect does not find mental representation, i.e., she *cannot imagine or visualize* a sense of comfort or ease. Her capacity to transform affectual stimulation into symbolic thinking, by finding words for her feelings, is derailed. (M)other cannot be reached, and therefore cannot be 'conceived of' or 'thought' . . . The "mother"—the *other*—remains an 'unknown thought'.

3   Kullman, A. (2007). The 'perseverant' personality: A pre-attachment perspective on the etiology and evolution of binge/purge eating disorders. *Psychoanalytic Dialogues*, 17(5): 705–732.

4   Aron, L. (2000). Self-reflexivity and the therapeutic action of psychoanalysis. *Psychoanalytic Psychology*, 17(4): 667–689.

5   Fonagy, P. & Target, M. (1997). Attachment and reflective function: Their role in self-organization. *Development and Psychopathology*, 9: 679–700.

6   Bion, W. R. (1962b). Learning from experience. In *Seven Servants: Four Works by Wilfred R. Bion*. Northvale, NJ: Jason Aronson, 1977, p. 57.

# food for thought[1]

AS MEGAN AND I CONTINUED our work together, Megan began thinking about her eating disorder in a totally different way. Far from being "just about food," she could see that her bulimia was comprised of intricately interwoven, 'undigestible' thoughts and feelings, all at war with each other on the battlefield of her body. Megan was amazed to discover that every one of her binge and purge episodes—whether once or multiple times a day—was preceded by a thought, feeling, or memory that overwhelmed her capacity to "think" it. Whether it was concern over a brief she needed to write, or a conversation with her father; whether it was feeling uncomfortable at a party, or elated by a compliment at work, every time *"something happened"*—bad or good, conscious or unconscious—'food thoughts', cravings, urges to starve or purge were all triggered, leaving her unable to think, and feeling like she was "losing her mind."

"Every single morning I wake up promising myself I'll be 'good'," Megan's frustration was evident in her voice. "I promise myself I'll only eat vegetables or I'll follow the latest diet in my running magazine. But then, *something happens*. Something always happens! This morning I only made it to 6:43 a.m. before I started bingeing. All I could think about was getting food and getting it in me as fast as I could. I swear, I feel like I *literally* lose my mind!"

"What is that *something* that happens?" I asked her.

"It can be *anything*," she replied, "or it can be *nothing*. Yesterday I managed to go almost the entire day without bingeing and purging, but then I got home from work and before I knew it I was eating anything I could get my hands on. I tell myself I'll only eat one M&M or a small salad, just to help me calm down or focus on whatever I'm trying to do. But the minute I put *anything* in my mouth, it's all over. All of a sudden there's nothing else in my mind and I just *have* to keep eating."

"It seems like you start out trying to help yourself focus or concentrate," I reflected, "but then once the food is inside you, you get yourself all tied up in knots and things get even more confused."

"Exactly!" Megan replied. "And then, I eat *even more* to try and get over the confusion and the anxiety! I just do not get what is wrong with me!"

I started to remind Megan about the progress she had made, but thought better of it. I knew that anything less than perfection had never felt good enough for her. While the frequency of her binge/purge cycles had been steadily declining, she still began every morning with her characteristic mantra: Today, she would be 'good'; she would plan her meals, go to the gym, focus on eating "mindfully" and "healthily." But sometimes within moments, as she thought about her day, or within hours, as her day began to overwhelm her, her resolve would slip away. The insistent voices in her mind would grow in intensity, her determination demolished by incessant cravings. Most evenings, when her husband Jon was not at home, she would make the rounds of fast-food stores and take-out counters, being careful not to frequent the same ones too often for fear her patterns would be recognized. She would load up on 'junk food'— foods she would never allow herself to 'keep in'—and start to binge while still in her car. While some days were better than others, she still felt helpless in the face of the 'food thoughts' and cravings that seemed to take over her mind at will, confiscating all rational thinking and compelling her to eat.

"You see!" Megan's eyes suddenly widened and she thrust her arms across her body, hugging her torso. "It's happening right now! Here I am talking to you and all of a sudden I started thinking about what I'm going to eat when I leave here. If I were at home right now, I'd be heading straight for the refrigerator!"

*Here it was!* I thought to myself: The sudden shift from thinking with her mind to 'thinking' with her body, happening right before our eyes!

Megan's sudden shift, from thinking with her mind to 'thinking' with her body is what I call '**dysensithymia**'. Dysensithymia, as I have conceived and developed it, is "an impairment in the ability to distinguish between felt-states or senses of the body and mind." A reflection of what I believe to be the failure of the mind and body to separate and differentiate *from each other* beginning with the earliest feedings, dysensithymia may account for such phenomena as:

• The replacement of normally intact thinking with 'food thoughts' in the face of distressing or overwhelming emotional experiences

- The conflation of internal or 'gut' feelings of longing, anxiety, sadness (and so forth), with sensations of hunger
- The inability to differentiate between the ingestion of toxic *emotional* elements and the ingestion of food or 'fat'
- The attempt at garnering emotional fortitude by eating (or not eating)
- The *literal* use of food for thought.

As I listened to Megan, my mind went on instant replay, scanning our conversation. What had we been talking about that could have triggered her sudden dysensithymic shift from thinking with her mind to 'thinking' with her body?

"I wonder if something just happened," I asked her, "a sudden 'something' that made you uncomfortable in some way."

Megan thought for a moment. "I think I just got anxious telling you all that," she said sheepishly.

"What about it made you anxious?" I asked her gently.

"It just makes me feel embarrassed and ashamed," she replied, her face reddening. "Like all the things I *act* like I am on the outside are really just a fraud."

"You know," she continued, after a few moments of silence, "I was just thinking about last night. The managing partner gave me an assignment related to this really important case involving one of our biggest clients. Jon was out of town, so I decided to stay late at the office and have dinner with my Dad to talk about the case. I was so excited about the assignment! I had a healthy meal and felt really good about the conversation. And I was really proud of myself because I had made it through an entire day without bingeing or purging. Then I went home and felt all this nervous energy, so I decided to start working on the brief. I had a pretty good idea of what I needed to write, but I kept getting more and more anxious. Before I knew it, I just *had* to eat. First I ate the leftover lasagna. That didn't work. Then I made macaroni and cheese. Then I ate ice-cream, then some M&M's. It was like I was *crazed. What! What* will work! *Nothing* did!"

I nodded, thinking how food held out so much promise, but inevitably disappointed her.

"So, then what happened?" I asked, wondering whether her conversation with her father had somehow dysregulated her.

"Well, I threw up," she said. "And then I felt calmer and was able to work for a while. Until it all started over again."

"Okay, let's think about this for a minute," I said, wanting to help Megan slow down and hone in on the individual elements of her experience. "The food started out being a *good* thing—something you thought would help you when your mind was becoming overwhelmed. But then it didn't work, so you threw it up."

Megan nodded in agreement.

"So how did this good thing suddenly become transformed into something bad?"

As Megan and I explored the nuances of her experience, she began to see how whenever *"something happened"* and her mind became overwhelmed by thoughts she wasn't able to 'think' or situations she wasn't sure how to handle, her mind would suddenly and "inexplicably" be overtaken by 'food thoughts' and the urgent need to relieve her chaotic state by eating. As the precipitating thought, feeling, or memory would replay itself over and over in the *background* of her mind, the *foreground* would become preoccupied with thoughts of food and eating—reflecting her still-immutable belief that relief could be found in the feeding. But even as the first sensations would fill her mouth, momentarily soothing the physical and emotional urgency, it would quickly become apparent that the food wasn't working: No matter how much she consumed, the distressing thoughts in her mind would not be deterred. As she turned from one food to another, and each one failed to relieve her chaotic state, the urgency would escalate:

*Quick . . . the lasagna . . . the pasta . . . the ice-cream . . . the chocolate . . . What? What will help?*

Megan would eat frantically, without regard to taste; her body would fill without consciousness of fullness. But despite all her efforts, the chaotic thoughts in her mind could not be metabolized by her body. The binge not only failed to provide her with a *solution* for her *original* distress, but it also left her body full and distorted. As her thoughts would turn to the expanding state of her body, the cacophony in her mind would shift to a new refrain:

*"Look what you've done, you shouldn't have eaten that, you are such a fraud, you are so fat; you are disgusting . . ."*

Like the 'unfiltered' milk of infancy, the food once again would become the *literal bearer* and *concrete* embodiment of Megan's uncontained toxic emotional distress. Entering into the 'toxic container' of her undifferentiated body/mind, the once-coveted 'good' food in this way would be transformed into 'bad'. But, paradoxically, this transformation was not without its benefits, for it also provided Megan with an apparent solution to her distress: While terrifying thoughts and feelings could not be "repressed, suppressed or made unconscious,"[2] to paraphrase W. R. Bion, terrifying *food* could be *physically* eliminated from her body.

Purging thus provided Megan with a means of physically evacuating the undigestible toxic elements in her mind by way of her body. Extreme forms of exercise, laxative abuse, and/or starvation dieting after a binge, or when she *couldn't* purge, served a similar purpose. But even as the emptiness at the end of the cycle provided her with a brief moment in time when she felt free of toxicity, the relief was short-lived. For as the still-unfiltered toxic thoughts and fears returned to the foreground of her mind, the whole cycle would begin again.

This transformational process, where good and urgently-needed food would turn into bad, occurred virtually instantaneously for Megan. The moment food entered into the 'toxic container' of her*self*, her mind would begin racing and the binge and purge would become a *fait accompli*. One extra pea, a 'forbidden' spoonful of salad dressing, was enough to trigger fearful thoughts of taking in toxicity she didn't know how to digest, literally or figuratively. Food thus evoked both a promise and a conditioned fear response in her: What she longed for, needed, and urgently sought after, even—or *especially*—in the absence of physical hunger, was also saturated with emptiness, shame, and the terrifying, perceived danger of 'gaining weight' and becoming toxically 'fat', (i.e., containing toxic elements in and on her body). Megan could not differentiate between physical and emotional hunger, between food that she needed for physical sustenance versus food that served an emotional need. *All* food had the potential, even the *probability*, of triggering the perseverative binge and purge cycle, and she saw most food as dangerous: Holding out the *promise*, it never delivered on the fulfillment of her needs. The futility of this cycle filled Megan with shame, and she saw every failure to avoid taking in food as a failure of herself.

Nevertheless, this cyclical pattern served a vital function in Megan's life: It was the way she had learned to *think*, to process and regulate her emotions, and she therefore held onto it with tenacity—for it had helped her survive. Eating substituted for the containing mother she had always longed for, for the elusive 'other' she yearned to be with, to share her inner life. When thoroughly enmeshed in her eating disorder, it was with food that she shared her most intimate moments, and by way of the binge and the subsequent purge that she often did her most intense thinking. At times, in fact, she found herself bingeing solely in order to have something to purge. It was thus not the food itself that was the objective, but rather the *evacuation* of her toxic state of mind that seemed to be relieved only by way of the physical release. As the initial triggering 'psychic event' continued replaying during the binge, solutions for her distress would often occur to her during the purge. The cycle was thus self-reinforcing, providing her with a means of working through her distressful states of mind, or thoughts that shamed her, without needing to expose them—or herself—to others.[3]

"So, what if we went back and thought about the 'anxious' feelings," I asked Megan. "Do you have any thoughts on what those were about?"

"I'm not sure," she replied, slowly. "Maybe it was that I didn't want you to be disappointed in me." She thought for another moment. "I feel that a lot in my life, not just with you. Like last night, I started out working on the brief, but then I kept getting more and more edgy. I always get so anxious when I have to submit something to the court. And then, when I started thinking about actually *being* in court, I got afraid that I'd be standing up in front of the judge and I wouldn't be able to argue the case, or that my mind would go totally blank. I just get so scared that I will do or say something that will embarrass me or my firm, and they'll be totally disappointed in me."

"This fear that you will do or say something wrong, or that you'll embarrass or disappoint the firm," I said, carefully fitting together the pieces, "what do you suppose that's about?"

"I'm sure it has to do with my father," Megan replied. "I've always been afraid of disappointing my father. In fact, truthfully, the only reason I went into law to begin with was that I didn't want to disappoint my father! All my life, he talked about how *I* was the one who was going to follow in his footsteps. Neither of my brothers had the least bit of interest in going into law. I was the youngest, his last hope for someone to take over the practice he built. I didn't want to disappoint him."

"What would happen if your father was disappointed?"

"Oh, God," Megan wiped away the tears that instantly sprang to her eyes. "I can hardly even think about that. If my *father* was disappointed in me, it would mean that I'm *nothing*. My mother was so unpredictable. It's like I didn't have to care that much about what she thought as long as I knew my father was in my corner. But if my *father* was disappointed in me; if *he* thought I was a fraud, all my doubts and fears would be true. I don't think I could even live with that."

Megan leaned forward, clasping her head in her hands. "Oh, God," she moaned, "I just have this hard lump in my gut. It makes me feel like throwing up."

Here it was again. The toxic and distressing feelings transformed into a toxic, visceral response—a literal *dysensithymic*, gut-reaction to the thoughts that were too much for Megan's mind to bear. Her body was stepping in, offering to rescue her from the painful feelings that by now had become as physical as they were emotional.

## Notes

1   Material in this chapter has previously been published in: Kullman, A. (2007). The 'perseverant' personality: A pre-attachment perspective on the etiology and evolution of binge/purge eating disorders. *Psychoanalytic Dialogues*, 17(5): 705–732. And previously in: Kullman, A. (1995). *The 'Autizoid' Personality and the Eating Disorder*. Unpublished Doctoral dissertation.
2   Bion, W. R. (1962b). Learning from experience. In *Seven Servants: Four Works by Wilfred R. Bion*. Northvale, NJ: Jason Aronson, 1977, p. 8.
3   Kullman, A (2007), The 'perseverant' personality: A pre-attachment perspective on the etiology and evolution of binge/purge eating disorders. *Psychoanalytic Dialogues*, 17(5): 705–732.

# the 'toxic container'

RICKY WAS HUNGRY. He had already eaten his entire lunch and it was just ten past recess. He laid his head on his desk, thoughts of the morning flooding his mind. He had cried again when his mother had dropped him off at school that morning. He couldn't bear the thought of another day of taunting by his classmates. His mother had gotten mad at him for making a scene, and Tyler had seen him cry and told the others that he was "a big fat baby," and they had all laughed. They always laughed. No doubt his father would call him a sissy again tonight, probably even hit him, when Mother told him what had happened. Why did she always have to tell on him, anyway? Ricky sighed. Maybe Steven would share his cookies at lunchtime. And Geraldine never finished what her mother gave her. Maybe he could tell Mrs. Holmes he'd forgotten his lunch and she'd arrange for him to eat in the cafeteria . . .

"Ricky!" Mrs. Holmes' terse voice snapped him to attention. "If you're sleeping in class again, I will gladly send you out to the track to run laps. Maybe that will keep you awake!"

Ricky's face turned bright red as the class broke into laughter. This was definitely not going to be a good day.

★   ★   ★

Twenty-five years later, I opened the waiting room door to find Rick—normally relaxed, with a charming smile brightening his blue eyes and now-chiseled face—sprawled on the armless chair, head back against the wall, arms and legs splayed out to the sides. He got up and wordlessly made his way into the consulting room.

"I blew it," he said, before I had a chance to sit down. "I blew it again. I am such a frigging moron. What the hell is wrong with me? Thirty pounds down and now probably ten back up. Overnight."

"What happened?" I asked, far more concerned about Rick's sudden display of self-hatred than the apparent lapse in his dieting. Though I knew this to be his umpteenth effort at losing the excess fifty pounds he had carried around since early childhood, I also knew that his lifelong struggle had little to do with his inability to stay on a diet. I listened carefully for connections as his story unfolded . . .

★   ★   ★

Rick bolted out the door of the Political Science building, the note he had received just moments before from the department head still clutched in his hand.

*What is so urgent*, he worried, as he headed for the faculty parking lot. *Why does she want to see me at 7:00 a.m. tomorrow morning?*

Rick's hands trembled as he fumbled with his keys, trying to unlock his truck.

"Calm down, calm down," he ordered himself aloud.

*Did someone file a complaint against me? Did I not get the promotion? Forget the promotion, did she decide not to renew my contract? What will I tell Jamie?*

Rick wove his truck through the parking lot, brakes squealing, swerving just in time to avoid hitting the small blue Honda that suddenly braked in front of him. He blasted his horn, glaring at the driver of the offending vehicle as he sped past.

"Oh, Lord," he groaned aloud, recognizing the head of the Political Science department. He slumped in his seat, embarrassment flooding his body and mind.

*"Just can't get it right, can you, boy?"* Rick could hear his father's accusatory tone as clearly as if the old man were sitting in the backseat of his truck. *"I always told your mother you'd make nothing of yourself."*

Rick dropped his chin to his chest, the ache in his gut sickeningly familiar. The oldest of five siblings, he never *had* figured out what it would take to please his violent, alcoholic father, who had never taken the risk of spoiling his children by sparing the rod. And his mother, who had grown more distant with the birth of each successive child, seemed to be as frightened of his father as were the children. Rick was frequently held responsible not only for his own misdeeds but for failing to keep his younger brothers and sisters in tow. Now, at thirty-five, he still was never quite sure which of his actions might spell disaster.

Rick inched his truck into the barely moving traffic, the tension in his body growing with each humiliating mental replay. Suddenly thoughts of french-fries invaded his mind: *French fries, with salt and ketchup.* He could taste them. *And maybe a triple cheeseburger with extra onions and sauce . . . and relish . . . and a real Coke . . .*

"No, no! Don't go there!" he berated himself. "*Thirty pounds. Don't blow it. Focus, damn it! Just focus. Breathe in, breathe out . . .*"

Rick swerved off the road and into the parking lot of the local Burger Time. The line at the drive-through was five-cars long. Pounding the steering wheel in frustration, he plowed back into traffic and headed for the mini-mart half-a-block up the road. He bought a family-size bag of potato chips and an extra-large diet soda.

"*Damn!*" he argued with his father's image, rapidly stuffing chips into his mouth. "*She stopped right in front of me! I had every right to be mad.*"

"*You're nothing but a fool, boy,*" his father's voice coldly retorted.

Rick spied the Taco Tico near the freeway, relieved to find the drive-through free of competing vehicles. He ordered the family special, estimating that ten tacos ought to be enough to get him home, especially if there wasn't too much traffic on the freeway.

Half an hour later, Rick greeted Jamie with a peck on the cheek. "Boy am I starving!" he announced, tossing his jacket onto the sofa and heading straight for the dinner table. He sat down to an eight-ounce steak, a large serving of broccoli, and a tossed green salad with fat-free Italian dressing. He tried to listen to Jamie's recital of the day's events—her visit to the OB's office, the shopping she had done for the baby's room—but worry about his job and their future distracted him. Cleaning his plate, he carried his dishes to the sink and opened the pantry. He slathered peanut butter and jelly on several pieces of wheat bread, stuffed his pockets with pistachio nuts and leftover Halloween candy, and, grabbing the pint of Rocky Road out of the freezer, headed for the family room.

Jamie followed, looking at him quizzically. "Uh, Rick . . ." she hesitated.

"Don't even go there!" he snapped.

Jamie's eyes filled with tears, and she fled upstairs. Rick cursed himself, but couldn't pry himself away from the food in front of him to follow her. He turned on the TV and stared blankly at the screen, barely aware of the constant movement of hand to mouth.

Rick awakened at 5:00 a.m. the next morning, still on the couch. He lumbered up the stairs, pausing to stare at himself in the hall mirror. His face looked flushed and bloated, the dark circles under his eyes more pronounced than ever. He felt sick, nauseated.

*Idiot! Fool!* He scowled at his reflection. *This has got to stop right now. You're going to skip breakfast and go straight to the gym right after the meeting.*

Rick stepped out of the shower and began readying himself for the dreaded encounter with his department head. He selected one of his new tailored dress shirts, noticing that the sleeves and collar felt oddly uncomfortable. The cleaners must have shrunk them, he thought to himself. Putting on the pants of his new blue suit, he was aghast when he could barely button the waistband. The jacket wasn't much better. He ripped off the clothing, leaving it in a heap on the closet floor. He pulled on a baggy sweater and sweat pants, gently kissed Jamie goodbye, and detouring to the kitchen, downed a huge glass of orange juice and buttered two bagels to take with him before heading out to the truck.

★   ★   ★

"You'd think I'd get it by now, wouldn't you?" Rick pounded his fist into his hand, avoiding my eyes. "I've been coming, what, two months now? I've been following all my damn diet guidelines, and I've been feeling so good! And then in ten seconds the whole thing is out the window! What the hell is wrong with me?"

It had indeed been two months, I calculated, since Rick had decided to return to his perennial high-protein-low-calorie diet plan—the one on which he had found repeated, if short-lived, success in the past—while we worked on the 'yo-yo' diet mentality that had brought him to the same critical juncture so many times before. I knew that his diet made him feel contained: Not having to think too much about what he was "allowed" to eat helped him feel more organized and in control. And watching the number on the scale drift downward most days reassured him that he was on the right track. But too much emphasis on how and what he should eat had worried me. Restrictive diets inevitably trigger feelings of deprivation and, even under the best of circumstances, rarely produce long-term results.

"Something sounds like it went wrong *for* you—not *with* you—yesterday," I reflected. "*Something* happened. What do you think that might have been?"

"It was the note," he replied, anger rising in his voice. "The damn note set me off. Why does that bitch do things like that? Why couldn't she just find me in the hallway and tell me what she wanted—or even put it in her damn note?"

"What was it about the note?" I asked. "And what do you think the connection was between the note and your sudden thoughts of french-fries and hamburgers?"

"Well . . ." Rick hesitated, his face reddening. "I guess it wasn't just the note. Maybe it was also what happened in the parking lot. I felt like such a fool." Rick shifted uncomfortably on the couch, defeat now evident in his voice. "Like such a failure. Here I am starting to make a name for myself in the Department, even on track to becoming an Assistant Professor, and then I blow it in one stupid outburst. I always ruin everything."

"*Did* everything get ruined?" I asked. "Did you find out what she wanted?"

Rick's face momentarily brightened. "Well, no," he grinned. "It didn't all actually get ruined. It all turned out fine—great, in fact. She wanted to know whether I would head up the anti-war rally and act as a liaison with the other departments." Rick's face fell again. "And she even apologized for what happened in the parking lot. *That* made me feel even more like a fool."

"How so?"

"Because I blew eight weeks of dieting for nothing!" he slapped his thigh again. "And now I'm back on the roller coaster. I started bingeing this morning even before I went out the door."

"So, it sounds like as long as things are working well, you are able to think, to keep focused on your eating and weight-loss goals," I suggested. "The problem arises when *something happens*. Something unexpected; something that seems like it blows the circuits in your mind."

"Exactly," Rick replied. "I just stop thinking. In that moment, nothing else matters. I'd have killed for a hamburger right then."

"How do you think a hamburger would have helped you?"

Rick considered my question. "Maybe I try to shut HIM up," he said. "It's like he sits in the back seat of my life and offers constant commentary. He thinks I'm an idiot and I believe him, even today."

I nodded, knowing well that what Rick called "the voice"—the conscious and unconscious chatter he carried around in his mind—wielded devastating power over his sense of himself. Children 'take in'—or *resist* taking in—what their parents put into them. If they are routinely fed love, security, and acceptance, they learn to process and regulate their emotions together with others and absorb a sense of their own worth. But if they are routinely fed ridicule, rage, disappointment, or punishment—or accused of being 'too selfish' or 'too sensitive'—they digest a sense of shame and humiliation that is absorbed into their systems as surely as the food on their plates. While lapses in connection are inevitable—anyone can get angry or disappointed sometimes—children who are subjected to prolonged, repeated, or painfully distressing interactions with the people they love and depend on, and/or are not provided the opportunity for repair of the broken connections, are left emotionally alone to try and contain their overwhelming feelings on their own. Like Rick, they become their own 'toxic containers',[1] holding and storing their distress inside themselves, forever in search of a way of 'evacuating'[2] it.

"So, did it work?" I asked him. "Did the food shut him up?"

"Yeah, right," Rick smirked. "For about ten seconds."

"And then what happened?"

"The second that junk was inside me, it was all over. I might as well just forget it."

"Forget it," I considered. "What did you tell yourself?"

"That I'm *an idiot, a fool, a fraud, a jerk, a failure, a nothing*," Rick pounded on his thigh again with each damning word.

"For wanting a hamburger?"

"Well, no," he said. "For being the kind of idiot who ate ten tacos and a ton of other junk when I'm on a diet and trying to lose twenty more pounds!"

I contemplated his words. "Or perhaps," I said slowly, "it is being the kind of person who tries so hard to be good, to get it right, but gets so overwhelmed by his own thoughts and feelings that he doesn't know what else to do with himself but eat."

Rick sat silently, thinking, for several minutes.

"That really is true about me," he said finally. "I really do try to be 'good'. To eat the right food, to do the right things, to be a good husband, to be the son my father could finally be proud of. But the truth is . . ." he stared down at the floor, "I just never feel good enough."

We walked silently to the door. "So, did your father win another round?" I asked quietly.

Rick stopped and looked at me. "What do you mean?" he asked.

"Every time you turn against yourself, you carry on your father's legacy," I observed. "It seems like you may be even harder on yourself than he was on you."

"Oh," he said. "I never thought about it like that."

Rick had spent his life trying to manage his own toxic feelings. Thoughts and feelings that overwhelmed his capacity to contain on his own were instantly replaced by 'food thoughts' and the urgent need to eat, only to be replaced yet *again* by an even more devastating set of toxic indictments. Even the most carefully thought-out diet plan and the best of intentions were no match for their powerful grip. Left on his own to process his emotions, Rick had carried around the weight of his father's judgments and the pain of his mother's emotional absence no matter how many diets he had attempted. Now, he still reached out to eat when his mind could contain no more. But his eating provided only momentary relief. In fact, the more he took in, the worse he felt. As his body grew full, the distress of the excess food became hopelessly intertwined with his own uncontained toxic emotion. Identified with that toxicity, Rick had come to see himself as bad and toxic.

"Perhaps you could give yourself a break, just a little slack," I suggested, as we reached the door. "Perhaps you could even think about treating yourself the way you wish your father had treated you—or the way you hope to treat that baby you have on the way."

Rick opened the door slowly, reluctant to leave.

"Okay," he said, and I sensed his armor loosening a bit. "I could think about that."

Perhaps it would be a better day after all.

★   ★   ★

Later, as my day drew to a close, I found myself thinking about Rick's escalating reactions, the 'food thought' and the urgency that suddenly took over his mind. How much they reminded me of Megan's struggle with bulimia. Despite the differences in their backgrounds and histories, even in their eating disorders, their thinking patterns were so similar. I knew that Rick's father—the focus of many of our sessions—had had little patience with his eldest son, as quick to deride him as he was to strike out. Nor was Rick's mother much of a buffer. While Rick had never questioned how much his mother loved him, he often described her as being withdrawn and depressed. Rick had seen pictures of his first year of life, the adoring way his mother had looked at him. But she had become more and more guarded with the birth of each successive child, and he had grown more alone.

As Rick grew older, things became even more complicated. Often turning to food to soothe himself, he was already quite overweight by the time he entered Kindergarten. He became the class clown, even joining the others in laughter while being teased about his weight. His teachers often felt compelled to complain to his parents about the disruptions he always seemed to be at the center of in class. Nevertheless, Rick had succeeded in getting through school, becoming the first member of his family to attend the state college. Working full time, he had completed his education, gotten married, was expecting a baby, and was even being considered for an assistant professorship. His yo-yo binge/dieting seemed to him to be the last vestige—and constant reminder—of his painful past.

As I continued thinking about the story he had told me, I could see that when Rick received the note from the head of the department, his mind had become flooded with fear and confusion: Notes from 'the teacher' had always heralded disaster. Without realizing it, Rick had not even allowed himself to share his concern with Jamie for fear she would react the way his mother had, or that he would damage her in some way. The next morning, when his clothes were tight and uncomfortable, the years of teasing and struggle he had endured as an overweight child were reawakened. But, clearly, he had few more resources to deal with his distress as an adult than he'd had as a child. Always fearful of his father's rage and his mother's disintegration, Rick had learned to keep his distressful feelings to himself. With no new input to help shift his perspective, the unmetabolized body/mind memories had become part of the emotional bank account in his mind. When *something happened* that triggered similar emotions, the synaptic connections in his brain fired their warnings along the same neuronal pathways, and his distress and confusion were instantly overshadowed by the 'food thoughts' that invaded his mind. French fries, hamburgers and bagels, along with the urgent need to consume them as quickly as possible, allowed his shame and the terrifying thoughts about his future to be temporarily stored on the back burner of his mind as he tried desperately to find a way to think about them. They were his body's way of helping him survive the emotional flooding he could barely allow himself to feel.

But if that were the case, I considered, why was Rick a yo-yo dieter, rather than suffering from bulimia like Megan? Re-playing his history in my mind, I thought about how Rick's body/mind memory had also inevitably recorded the special times he had shared with his mother before the births of his younger siblings. He had learned about and experienced 'taking in' from those times, discovering that he 'existed' in his mother's heart and mind, that he impacted her and was deserving of her responses. Consciously and unconsciously, he had held on to the memory of her nurturing before she had become fearful and distracted. Rick's yo-yo dieting reflected this cyclical feast-and-famine pattern. When in distress, he would reach out for his mother's comforting good food, the nurturance he once knew having become encoded in his unconscious memory. These early positive experiences had helped him achieve certain developmental milestones—not the least of which was the capacity to *wait*—to delay gratification—that evolves with the repeated experience of mother reliably reappearing after an absence. Rick had learned from his earliest experiences that, if he waited long enough, his distress would find relief. But as his history as an overweight child revealed, this calculation had not stood the test of time. Waiting for "the other half of the meal"—the nurturance—had soon become a full-time and futile exercise. The toxic feelings stored in his body as he waited had manifested in his lifelong battle with his weight. And the dieting he engaged in, which served as the periodic purge of his toxicity, was his unconscious acknowledgement of paradise lost.

Megan, on the other hand, had not developed this capacity to wait. Her life had been fraught with conflict and anxiety from the start, her mother distracted by endless pressures and bearing her own history of neglect. In a sense, Megan had never known where her next emotional meal might be coming from or what it might contain. Would her mother be happy with her or indifferent, open to playing or eager to get the feeding over with? Would her father tweak her braids or act disappointed in her? The emotional milk had been sweet on some occasions and curdled on others. Over time, Megan had become increasingly overwhelmed, barely able to tolerate the painful and conflicted feelings inside her, their presence indistinguishable from the full and uncomfortable feelings she felt when she took in too much food. Left to process these toxic feelings on her own, without an emotional partner to help her think them through, she, too, had served as her own 'toxic container', identifying with the toxic feelings inside her and seeing herself as bad and toxic. These unresolved toxic feelings had become the source of her body dysmorphia—her body-image distortions, low self-esteem, and self-hatred. At times Megan had binged and purged more than twenty times a day, unable to tolerate these undifferentiated toxic elements inside her for more than a few moments at a time. For her, the binge reflected the hope, the promise, the possibility of relief, only to have the food turn toxic the moment it entered into her body/self.

Turning off the lights and locking the door, I thought about how each one of the perseverant eating disorders can be 'read', understood, and even serve as a blueprint for the psyche. Whether a cyclical eating disorder plays itself out in the form of purging/bulimia, compulsive eating, or yo-yo binge/dieting, the body is trying to help process emotions that overwhelm the mind. When, in the absence of physical hunger, Rick's or Megan's or millions of other people's minds are suddenly overtaken by 'food thoughts' and the compulsion to eat, they are receiving a clear message that whatever they are doing, thinking, or feeling is causing them distress. And when they find themselves in the midst of a binge, a purge, or yet another diet, they have crossed over the edge of being able to *think through* whatever is going on in their minds, and have begun reaching for help and hope in the food.

## Notes

1   Kullman, A. (1995). *The 'Autizoid' Personality and the Eating Disorder.* Unpublished Doctoral dissertation. See also Kullman, A. (2007). The 'perseverant' personality: A pre-attachment perspective on the etiology and evolution of binge/purge eating disorders. *Psychoanalytic Dialogues*, 17(5): 705–732, 714.
2   Bion, W. R. (1962b). Learning from experience. In *Seven Servants: Four Works by Wilfred R. Bion.* Northvale, NJ: Jason Aronson, 1977, pp. 1–111, p. 13.

# the 'closed-circuit loop'

THE URGENCY IN SUSIE'S VOICE concerned me. Though I had been seeing her for almost a year, she had never before called between sessions. Now, in the hour since I had last checked, four messages had preceded her frantic phone call:

"*Please*, I'm late for my appointment and I was getting ready to go and I threw up into my container and it spilled over and it got all over the walls and the carpet and *everything* and I don't know what to do! *Please*, could you call me as soon as you can and help me! Help me figure out what I should do, how I can clean it up?"

I called Susie's number, but there was no answer. She must be on her way. A sense of relief washed over me that she was alright, along with a slight sense of encouragement. Susie had indeed sounded desperate, but rather than staying isolated and hidden—her usual pattern—she had reached out to me to help her think through her distressing situation. We were making progress.

The light indicating Susie's arrival finally lit up in my office. I opened the waiting room door to find her sitting stiffly in her chair, hands clasped in her lap, looking despondent.

"I'm sorry I didn't get your message in time," I said, wondering how my failure to be there when she reached out for me might play itself out.

"That's okay," she replied glumly, making her way into the consulting room. "I figured out how to clean up *that* mess. But I think it happened in the first place because I've been so frazzled and upset. I've had an absolutely *horrible* weekend."

As Susie settled on the couch, I recalled that she had planned to go to her home state over the weekend for a family reunion.

"It just doesn't work anymore," she finally said.

"What doesn't work?"

"Just *everything*," she replied. "Acting cute; the whole way I've lived my life. It's like *everything* is spilling over and causing huge messes."

"Did something happen at the reunion?"

"Talk about a disaster," Susie shook her head. "I was such a stupid mess there."

I winced at Susie's self-deprecating comments, but knew better than to try and contradict them. Like so many of my perseverant patients, Susie was a storehouse of negative beliefs about herself. Our painstaking effort at working them through was still a work in progress.

"Everyone used to just pinch my cheeks and tell me how cute I was," she mourned, "but this time was different. My mother was hardly speaking to me because I arrived late and kept everyone waiting. My grandmother was *awful*. She kept asking me all these questions about whether I have a boyfriend and why I'm not married. And my aunt and uncle! I overheard them talking about me, saying I never finished college and that I was still working at a minimum wage job! How did they even *know* that? Has my mother been talking about me behind my back? But . . ." Susie continued, reaching for another tissue, "the *really* worst part was my sister. I was just *standing* there," she sputtered, "and we were talking to my cousins, and I don't even remember what I said. But all of a sudden, my sister Samantha turned on me and *dragged* me into the kitchen and started screaming at me: '*Don't you ever* think *before you speak!*'"

Susie's whole body was wracked with sobs.

"Samantha wouldn't even *speak* to me for the rest of the weekend," she said when she could breathe again. "And my mother wouldn't have anything to do with me either. And I didn't even know what I did. All my sister would say was that everyone was rolling their eyes and I was too stupid to even notice it. She said that I had embarrassed her for the last time and she was sick of it. I could barely make it through the party," her voice quivered. "I spent most of the weekend in my room bingeing and purging. All I could think about was how no matter how hard I try I always make a mess of everything."

Susie wept.

As I sat with Susie, absorbing her grief, I could feel how greatly she suffered as she had tried to navigate her way through her emotional world. Susie had worked hard to present an outward appearance of 'normalcy' by mimicking the actions of others, all the while living in a world she did not emotionally understand. Her need to 'evacuate' the confusing contents of her mind were often met with resistance or disdain by those who could not comprehend the urgency of her distress. Susie struggled with feelings of humiliation every time she attempted any interaction with others, fearing she might reveal the innermost contents of her mind and everyone would know how "worthless" and "stupid" she was. At the same time, she could not discern the genuine interest others expressed in her, not believing that anyone could find her interesting. Susie agonized for hours, often in a haze of bingeing and purging, perseverating over every word or nuance exchanged. Her deepest organizing principle was a belief that others had no interest in her and would inevitably reject her, much as happened in her relationships with her family.[1]

Susie's confusion about how the world works was perhaps best symbolized by her dyslexia. In the course of my years of practice, I have been struck by what appears to me to be an unusually high percentage of eating-disorder patients who report histories of diagnosed (or undiagnosed) learning disabilities, and/or confusion about the 'rules' of social interaction usually taken for granted by others. Research has shown that people with language-based learning disabilities spend an inordinate amount of time concentrating on each and every syllable, attending to *every* sight and sound with equal attention and concentration.[2] In similar fashion, Susie appeared to have both the fortune and misfortune of seeing the world in ways others did not, a three-dimensional perspective, as it were, on her environment and the 'objects' (literal and figurative) in it. In what I think of as '**emotional/relational dyslexia**', Susie had a perseverative *over-investment* in the nature, nuance, and meaning of interpersonal modes of communication and relatedness. Engaging in what I call '**relational rumination**' she had an intense desire to *know*, to read between the lines of meaning, to decode or deconstruct the emotional undercurrents of every interaction and communication. She perseverated over every perceived slight or miscommunication and felt humiliated when she didn't "get" what other people seemed to easily intuit. Susie was dogged by indecisiveness— how to *be*, how to *act*. And when finally overwhelmed by her circuitous efforts at deciphering such 'undigestible' or dysregulating situations or communications on her own—be they positive or negative—her mind would become flooded with familiar surges of 'food thoughts', replacing all her usable thinking with the urgent need to eat.

This repetitive or perseverant pattern of reaching for connection via the feeding had remained encoded in Susie's brain circuitry—the mind/body memory she carried with her throughout her lifetime: When she experienced distress, she reached out for the feeding; when the feeding failed to help her, she reached out again. Unconsciously reliving her quest for emotional connection by way of the feeding, Susie spent hours in the fog of eating, the food itself of far less importance than the ongoing, rhythmic motion of repeatedly filling her mouth—resurrecting the hope of being simultaneously fed and cared for, as she had been at least for a while in infancy. Caught in the 'closed-circuit loop' of psychic and somatic perseveration[3] that had fueled her lifetime of eating disorders, Susie's ability to think about her emotional experiences was repeatedly supplanted by her desperate attempt at *concretely* eliminating her overwhelming feelings.

With all this underlying chaos, self-regulation was an ongoing challenge for Susie. She didn't know how to rest, how to soothe her own emotional states, how to transition from one activity to another without eating to quell the chaos. She had developed a cadre of rhythmic, self-regulating strategies— crossed-legged kicking, rocking, hair-pulling, face-picking—physical enactments that mirrored the intensity of her emotional perseveration and distress. Susie made endless lists and counted everything. She did things in prescribed sequences and had 'rules' defining what she was allowed and not allowed to do. She would only eat things that came in 'units': A whole sandwich or a bag of cookies was a unit; a 'piece' of cake was not a unit and therefore could not be eaten. These rules, we came to understand, provided her with the sense of structure and sequencing her childhood had not. She saw these requirements as providing "boundaries" for herself. They made her feel safe, able to be counted on to stay consistent in the otherwise confusing emotional world she tried to navigate on her own.

Children perseverate, observed infant and child researchers Stanley I. Greenspan and Serena Wieder, (a) because it is reassuring to do what is familiar, and (b) because they have difficulty sequencing, or knowing how to move on to something else.[4] Sequencing is a developmental task normally achieved in the first year of life. An otherwise healthy infant whose needs are regularly attended to becomes accustomed to eating, sleeping, and playing at regular intervals, quickly coming to expect, and then internally predict, what comes next. This sense of regularity helps the child organize her internal experience, as well as her expectations of the external world. But if a child experiences continuous inconsistencies, her sense of what happens next may remain tenuous. As she grows older, she may have difficulty organizing herself, moving from one activity to another, or following through on tasks or ideas in an orderly or sequential manner. If, like Susie, she never learns that change can be successfully managed, she may become frightened or alarmed at its prospect.

Living life in such a hypersensitive state had brought years of distress to Susie. She took things too literally, her parents and sisters argued. She was far too sensitive. She needed to "chill out," to "pour a bottle of oil down her back and let things slide off." Susie knew her vulnerability showed and she remembered the years of taunting she had painfully experienced in childhood. Yet she could do nothing to stop herself from the perseveration that both fueled, and was fueled by, the eating disorder that foreclosed all her other thinking.

"Are you sure that your cousins reacted to you in the same way your sister did?" I asked her when her tears subsided.

"I didn't think so at first," she replied, blowing her nose. "Not until Samantha said that they were rolling their eyes."

"Do you think it's possible that Samantha was mistaken?"

Susie looked at me. "Well, two of my cousins *did* come up to me later in the evening to talk and everything seemed just normal," she replied. "I think it's a lot easier for me to talk when there isn't a whole group of people. That gets me all anxious and turns me into a 'motor-mouth', like Samantha said."

"What did your cousins talk to you about?"

"They wanted to know what I was up to, what my life in California was like, stuff like that."

"Did you feel like they were making fun of you?"

"No, not at all." Susie sat quietly for a few moments. "Actually, I felt pretty good while I was talking to them—like I wasn't such a fool."

"You know, Susie," I said quietly, "the reunion sounds like it was really difficult for you. I think it is very understandable that you would have needed some support. I wonder if you sensed something in Samantha beforehand that made you anxious even before you started talking."

Susie looked over at me, surprised. "That *is* exactly what happened," she said. "I didn't even think of that. It's like Samantha is always on edge, always expecting me to embarrass her or something. It just makes me feel self-conscious and even more nervous."

"You are so used to being thought of and treated like a problem," I reflected. "I can see how uncomfortable that would make you."

Susie was pensive. But in her next words I could hear how the support I had offered had allowed her to reconsider thoughts and feelings that, just moments before, had been too painful for her to bear.

"The truth is," she said, "that when I get anxious, I probably *do* talk too much or too loud or in circles—and maybe people really *do* roll their eyes.

It's like I'm even sort of aware of it when it's happening, but I can't stop myself."

Susie was silent for another moment. "So maybe I need to be more aware of it, huh?" she looked at me intently.

"Maybe," I smiled. "But mostly, I think you may need to be a little kinder and gentler with yourself, a little more patient and forgiving. Relating is hard work."

Susie nodded. She inhaled deeply as she stood up, as if fortifying herself to go out one more time to face the world.

After Susie left, I thought back to her telephone call that morning—the first contact she had ever initiated outside her analytic hours. The symbolism in her message was inescapable: Unable to regulate the intense emotion that had been stirred-up by her weekend, she first turned to food in an effort at helping herself think. She then attempted to 'evacuate' the overwhelming and 'undigestible' toxic elements by purging into her 'container', which, by spilling over, had finally proven itself incapable of 'containing' her. For the first time, Susie had been able to reach out to me and ask for help in "cleaning it up," that is, in finding a link where we could think together and find a solution for her distress. Susie's solitary and circular pattern had finally been interrupted, brought into a 'third'[5] dimension that included a living 'other'. Susie had allowed me to serve as her 'psychic container'—one who could help her hold and transform her terror and learn to channel her chaos into thoughts she could use for thinking.[6]

We had achieved a milestone.

## Notes

1   For the original discussion of this crucial moment in Susie's case, See Kullman, A. (2007). The 'perseverant' personality: A pre-attachment perspective on the etiology and evolution of binge/purge eating disorders. Psychoanalytic Dialogues, 17(5): 705–732, 719.
2   Tallal, P., Merzenich, M., Miller, S., & Jenkins, W. (1998). Language learning impairments: Integrating basic science, technology and remediation, Experimental Brain Research, 123: 210–219.
3   Kullman, A. (2007).
4   Greenspan, S. & Wieder, S. (1998). The Child with Special Needs: Encouraging Intellectual and Emotional Growth. Reading, MA: Perseus Books, pp. 148–149.
5   Ogden, T. H. (1994). The analytic third: Working with intersubjective clinical facts. International Journal of Psychoanalysis, 75: 3–19.
6   Watillon-Naveau, A. (1992). Alice or the vicissitudes of the mother-daughter relationship. International Review of Psychoanalysis, 19: 209–216.

# *no words to say it*

"MY MOTHER CALLED last night," Megan began her session. "Oh?" I replied. "It's been a while, hasn't it?"

"Twelve weeks," she said, barely a glimmer of emotion in her voice. "Actually, twelve weeks and three days. I hate it when she does this. I think this is the longest time ever."

A shudder ran through my body. This surely wasn't the first time a patient had told me that her mother had stopped talking to her, but it never failed to unsettle me. While lapses in connection are inevitable, such extended breaches in emotional connection had undoubtedly had significant consequences for Megan over the years—not the least of which was a profound sense of isolation, shame, and the need to process her experiences on her own.

"She got mad at me at Christmas," Megan continued, matter-of-factly. "Of course, I didn't *know* she was mad at me until I called her two days later and she wouldn't take my call. Naturally, I didn't know what I did—and she wouldn't tell me."

"You're sounding like this is all quite routine," I noted. "Sort of like you just take it in your stride."

"Oh, I'm used to it," Megan said, a bit too nonchalantly. "At least I *should* be used to it. This is how she's always been. All of a sudden, she's not talking to me. She does it with my brothers and my Dad, too. I think it runs in her family. She and my grandmother aren't speaking to each other half the time, and there's always *someone* on the outs with my aunts and uncles."

"What was that like for you?" I asked.

Megan hesitated. "I think it was always hardest on me," she said, and I began to sense a resurgence of emotion in her. "My brothers never seemed to care much whether she was talking to them or not, but I would get really upset. I'd beg her to talk to me. I'd ask her questions, try to get her to respond. I'd tell her I had a project for school, or that I would cook dinner, but she would just ignore me, like I wasn't even in the room. If there was something I really needed, I'd have to ask my dad. It was like I was *dead* to her."

Megan paused, seeming to relive a memory.

"I never knew when it was going to happen," she said. "Sometimes I would say or do something that I was sure would make her mad, but she would just let it go or send me to my room. But other times, something would happen and she would just shut down. I couldn't reach her, no matter what I did. It was like she didn't even *know* me. No love, no care, *nothing*."

My mind was instantly alerted by Megan's words—the familiar phrase she and so many of my perseverant eating disorder patients used to characterize the onset of a binge: *Something happened*—something seemingly unknown and unknowable. I imagined what it must have been like for her to lose her sense of connection to her mother, especially during the early, formative years of her life: The emptiness, the absence, the "*nothing*" she had tried all her life to fill with food.

"And then," Megan's demeanor darkened, "it would be over. Like last night, she just calls and starts talking as if *nothing* has happened, as if we had all been away on vacation or something and we just needed to pick up where we left off."

Megan's mother didn't know how to find her way back, I thought to myself. She didn't know how to talk about what she was feeling, or engage in shared dialogue to work through and resolve issues together. Her own life experiences had clearly taught her to shut down and cut off when she was flooded with emotion, only later trying to bring herself back by 'picking up where she left off', and avoiding conflict. Unspoken, unresolved feelings everywhere. What stunning ramifications this must have had for countless generations of her family—as it clearly had had for her and Megan. Megan not only had lost out on the opportunity to understand what her mother was feeling, but also to find meaning and expression for her own internal states.

"What would your dad be doing while all this was going on?" I asked.

"My dad wasn't much help," Megan twirled a strand of her long, dark hair around her index finger. "He'd start out listening to me, but then it would just fall apart and he'd start lecturing me: '*Think about how your mother feels, Megan*'," she mimicked her father's tone. "'*What have you done to make her so angry? You should be thinking about what she feels, not just about yourself*'."

"Ouch," I said. "How did *that* leave you feeling?"

"*Awful*," she replied. "And it was so not true! I *always* worried about what they thought. Talking to my dad just made me feel *worse*."

I started to ask Megan what "worse" felt like, but she quickly continued with a memory: "There was this one time—I must have been about eight or nine years old—and we were staying in a cottage at the beach. My parents had been fighting all day. All of a sudden, my father came storming out of the bedroom, took me by the arm and said—'Come on, Megan, let's go to the beach.' My mother came storming after him, looked at me, and her eyes warned, *'Don't you dare go.'* I still remember the feeling of terror, of not knowing what to do. Would my father be mad at me if I didn't go? Would my mother be mad if I *did?* Which would be worse?"

"So, what did you do?"

"I went with my father."

"Because . . .?"

"I guess because I felt like I was safer with him," she replied. "I think it was scarier to think about *him* being mad at me than my mom. She might not talk to me, but I couldn't risk losing my dad."

I listened carefully to Megan's answer, aware that she didn't realize how she had actually felt safer with her mother—more willing to take a risk with her, less fearful of losing her than she was of losing her father.

"But in the end," she continued, "I don't really know *which* was worse. I felt sick the whole time, knowing I would be in trouble with my mother when I got home."

"And were you?"

"Oh *yeah*," she declared. "Dead cold silence. She didn't talk to me for two weeks after that."

"Oh my," I said, commiserating. "So, did you feel like you had made the wrong decision?"

"No, not really," she said. "I probably would do the same thing again today."

"So, your mother's 'dead cold silence' felt more tolerable to you than risking the loss of your father's approval."

"Yes," Megan hesitated. "But with my father, it was different. The silences with my mother were awful, but when they were over, they were over. Things went back to 'normal'—if you can call it that. She took me to practices or piano lessons, and always stayed to watch. And when she wasn't mad at me, things were okay. It was more what she *didn't say* when she stopped talking to me that felt so awful. But with my father. . . . He never stopped talking to me; he would just get . . . well, formal or *distant*, I guess. It's hard to put a finger on it. And he could say the most hurtful things and then later act like they didn't mean anything at all."

"How so?"

"Well, like last weekend," she said, "I got together with him for brunch to review my case. I wasn't dressed for work; I had just thrown something on. From the minute he saw me, I felt like he was looking me over. Finally, he said to me, 'I see you like blue dresses'."

Megan looked over at me. "That's it!" she exclaimed. "'*I see you like blue dresses*'! What does that even *mean*?! Does that mean he *likes* blue dresses, or he *doesn't* like blue dresses, or he doesn't like blue dresses on *me*, or he thinks I look fat and ugly in this *particular* blue dress? How am I even supposed to *think* about a comment like that!"

"Hmmm," I replied. "I see what you mean. Did you ask him what he meant?"

"Yes, as a matter of fact I did! And do you know what? He got all defensive! First, he asked me what *I* meant. Then he said that he hadn't meant anything at all, that he was just making an observation. He said it was *nothing* and that I'm always too sensitive and take things too literally. But I couldn't get it out of my mind all week."

Megan changed positions on the couch, suddenly looking particularly fragile.

"Then there's this other time that keeps coming to my mind," she said slowly, an unmistakable shadow descending across her face. "I can't remember what I did, but it was obviously something that really made him mad. He got right up in my face and started screaming at me, '*Who the hell do you think you are? You're nothing! You're nothing!*'"

Megan took a deep breath. "I've never forgotten those words." She reached for a tissue. "It may sound strange," she dabbed at her eyes, "but I really don't think he meant it, or that he really *believed* that about me. It's more like he just *flung* the words at me because he was mad. They weren't really supposed to *mean* anything beyond that moment. I brought it up to him a couple of years later and he said he thought I was crazy for carrying it around for so long. But I've never forgotten them to this day."

There are words, I thought to myself, and there are '*no*' words; and then there are words that cut to the quick. There are words that manipulate, words that aren't supposed to count, words never forgotten. Under the best of circumstances, words capture meaning. They give form and substance to the otherwise unformulated experiences that churn inside us. Babies begin developing language when their mothers put words to what they imagine they are feeling. A toddler focuses on 'me' and 'mine' as she learns the words that refer to, or distinguish between, what is on the inside of her and what is on the outside; what is 'of' her, and what is 'of' others. As a child comes to recognize and assign meaning to the same words she hears over and over again, her sense of herself and others comes to be defined within this shared symbolic system. The ability to identify feelings, to find and make use of words to describe them, and then to share them with others are essential ingredients of a "containing" emotional connection.

"It's as if he was saying that words don't *represent* anything," I said to Megan now. "They aren't supposed to contain or convey real meaning, or express thoughts and feelings that really matter. They're just supposed to mean . . . *nothing.*"

Megan's father's words were layered with multiple meanings for her. They carried a history—one that had left her bewildered by sudden 'shots in the dark', blindsided and made self-conscious by intrusions that disrupted her ordinary thinking and flooded her mind with confusion. Such projections had left her questioning herself, her feelings and perceptions, her decisions, opinions and inclinations—the very contents of her own mind. Did words have meaning or didn't they? Ought she believe what he said, or read between his lines to fathom what he meant? It wasn't simply that she wished for her father's approval—though surely that was true. It was that his sudden, unexpected outbursts and innuendos—not unlike her mother's sudden silences—had left her adrift, terrifyingly alone, without a shared language to help her make sense of her world. Now, Megan struggled with meaning, with "what to take in and what not to take in;" with who and how she was. She struggled to identify what reflected her own inner self-states and what reflected the psychic states of others.

"You know," Megan said a moment later, "my father can deliver a closing argument to a jury that would bring tears to your eyes. But then you go into the back room of the courthouse and he'll say, *'I really got to them, didn't I!'* It's like it's all a game to him. He has all the words in the world and he knows how to use them and manipulate people with them, all the while looking like the most sincere guy in the world. I don't think I've ever realized how much this has all affected me."

Megan paused for a long moment, deep in thought.

"It's sort of like my jeans," she said finally.

I looked at her quizzically. "Your jeans?"

"Yes," she said. "I've always thought my father telling me that I'm 'nothing' didn't mean that much or really have an effect on me. But I just realized that it's just like the size zero jeans I'm terrified to get rid of. I only feel like I'm *something* if I'm a size zero. As soon as my size zero jeans feel tight, I panic. I can't even go out. I feel like I'm *nothing*."

My mind scrambled, trying to follow the connections Megan was making. Suddenly I caught on to her living metaphor:

"Ah!" I replied. "It's like the only way you can be *something* is to be *nothing*, to be a zero—just like your father said you were."

"Yes!" Megan visibly relaxed. "That's it!"

"I can see the dilemma," I said. "How do you give up being a *zero*—a *nothing*—when 'nothing' is what you still believe you ought to be?"

Megan nodded, and again fell silent for several minutes.

"I was just thinking about what happened in the rest of the conversation with my mother," she said. "I responded like I always do: I answered her questions; I added some tidbits of my own. Anything, just to keep her talking, just to keep her with me."

"You've learned that you are supposed to act as if *nothing* has happened," I reflected. "I wonder whether that isn't the moment at which your 'thinking' brain freezes over and 'food thoughts' jump in instead."

Megan looked at me, surprised. "Exactly," she said. "I started eating even before I got off the phone. If there was any thinking going on before that, it all went out the window."

Megan wasn't dyslexic like my patient Susie, but she could have been. She was palpably aware of and frustrated by the 'holes' or deficiencies in her capacity to use her thoughts for thinking in moments of distress. As W. R. Bion had noted in the 'uncontained' individual, she felt baffled by the feelings and 'sense impressions' she could feel, but not make sense of.[1] While many patients with perseverant eating disorders struggle with with what Peter Sifneos called "alexithymia"[2]—lacking the words to describe their feelings— or what Joyce McDougall called "disaffectation"[3]—the "inability to contain and reflect over an excess of affective experience,"[4] Megan clearly had the capacity to express herself in words, to reflect on her emotional experiences, as well as a strong desire to know and think together with others. Nor was hers a problem with imagination: She had never lacked the ability to envision or creatively anticipate experiences.

Megan struggled with what I think of as '*dys-lexi-thymia*'—and define as an "impairment in the ability to make use of language and its nuances to capture the essence of, extract meaning from, and/or make emotional connection with the words assigned to experiences." Megan struggled with thinking and feeling at the same time, with the ability to perceive, let in, or sense what words and feelings meant or *felt like*. Her difficulty in connecting meaning with language had conspired to make her mind flee, to freeze, only to be taken over by the 'food thought' that replaced her capacity to think. Caught between the concealed and/or confused messages relayed by her parents, Megan wasn't sure what reflected her own inner states of being and what reflected the psychic states of others. When words didn't match or coincide with the unspoken messages they conveyed, '**dyslexithymia**' ensued and meaning disintegrated. Lacking the benefit of shared modes of thinking, language, and meaning, Megan had been locked inside her own pre-verbal (and *proverbial*) 'tower of babble' (*Babel*).

Might this 'confusion of tongues', I wondered—dual-messages that disrupted normal thinking—*underlie* alexithymia and disaffectation, leaving susceptible uncontained children and perseverant individuals without words to express, describe, or even experience the emotions they feel? And might not the continual state of cognitive/emotive confusion that I term 'dyslexithymia' evolve in the mind of the perseverant infant well before words develop—perhaps even be the *precursor* to such alexithymic states? In investigating the root causes of alexithymia, E. Lemche et al. found that "securely attached children rapidly acquired emotion, physiology, cognition and emotion-regulatory language, whereas insecurely attached and disorganized children either completely lacked internal-state language or displayed a considerable time-lag in the use of emotion and cognition vocabulary." Lemche et al. concluded that "The results raise the possibility that alexithymia might be a consequence of deficits in the development of internal-state language in the context of insecure or disorganized childhood attachment relationships."[5]

Megan had absorbed her father's words and her mother's silences, swallowed them whole. They remained undigested and unmetabolized, unconsciously and concretely enacted by way of her eating disorder.

As Megan gathered her things, I thought about how her mother's silences and her father's carelessness with words and meanings had left her without words or labels for emotions. Words provide the context; they are the building blocks of thinking. But while Megan had learned the basic names for feelings, she had missed out on the nuances of emotional expression. When words had been abused, misused, or withheld, she had not been able to learn how to connect what she experienced inside herself with the meaningful symbols of language. Instead, whenever "something happened," an avalanche of emotions would envelop her, leaving her suspended in emotional chaos, only to disintegrate into a physical act—a binge—the only way she knew to relieve the emotional turmoil within. In times of stress or distress, Megan could not "think with her thoughts"[6] or find strength or solace in connection with others. She couldn't use words to frame her experience. She could only eat.

## Notes

1  Bion, W. R. (1962b). Learning from experience. In *Seven Servants: Four Works by Wilfred R. Bion*. Northvale, NJ: Jason Aronson, 1977, p. 18.

2  Sifneos, P.E. (1973). The prevalence of 'alexithymic' characteristics in psychosomatic patients. *Psychotherapy and Psychosomatics*, 22(2): 255–226.

3  McDougall, J. (1989). *Theaters of the Body: A Psychoanalytic Approach to Psychosomatic Illness*. New York: W. W. Norton.

4  Ibid., p. 94.

5  Lemche, E., Klann-Delius, G., Koch, R., & Joraschky, P. (2004). Mentalizing language development in a longitudinal attachment sample: Implications for alexithymia. *Psychotherapy and Psychosomatics*, 73(6): 366–374, p. 366.

6  Bion, W. R. (1962b). Learning from experience. In *Seven Servants: Four Works by Wilfred R. Bion*. Northvale, NJ: Jason Aronson, 1977, p. 84.

# the shadow of shame

MACKENZIE WAS THE YOUNGEST of four children, born to middle-class working parents. She was an "accident," she had been told, conceived when her father had been home on leave from the war. Mackenzie had always known that her mother hadn't wanted any more children. Her mother had had little patience for her—the "extra" child who didn't fit into her plans to further her career. But when her father returned from his final tour of duty, he was delighted with this new baby daughter. He set up a home-based business and eagerly offered to take on responsibility for Mackenzie's care. Everyone knew that Mackenzie was Dad's favorite, a source of great irritation for her mother and resentful taunting by her older siblings. Nevertheless, Mackenzie had loved being the center of her father's attention—a fact that later came to haunt her.

When Mackenzie was just six years old, her father's special attention and tender embraces began to change. For the next seven years, he engaged Mackenzie in intimate touching every afternoon while her mother was still at work. Mackenzie recalled having a vague sense that something was wrong with what they were doing, but her time with her father seemed so loving, such a respite from her mother's harsh resentment. Still, as she grew older, Mackenzie's sense of guilt and shame grew. One afternoon she tried to tell her mother what was going on, but her mother reacted with rage, accusing Mackenzie of making up the story to cause trouble between her and Mackenzie's father.

By the time she turned thirteen, Mackenzie had become overtly rebellious and seriously bulimic. Taken to therapy, the secret relationship with her father was revealed. Finally convinced that the story was true, Mackenzie's mother was outraged and immediately filed for divorce. The therapist, as required by law, reported the abuse to authorities, and Mackenzie's father received the mandated sentence. After the trial, Mackenzie refused to have anything to do with her father. She moved out of the family home and maintained an ongoing, if tenuous, relationship with her mother and older siblings. In the end, however, her mother never followed through on the divorce. When her father was released from prison, her parents resumed their lives together and Mackenzie was again left to struggle with the meaning of the triangulation, competition, and boundary violations that had characterized her early life.

Fifteen years later, when Mackenzie came to me seeking help for her eating disorder, she had been slicing small lines into her arms with safety pins, the sight of the blood helping to calm her down. She didn't want to die, she told me, and I believed her; she just didn't know how to live. She saw herself as bad, toxic, poisonous. She wanted to live, but didn't believe she deserved to live; she wanted to love, but didn't understand how or why she loved the people who had abused her. A being such as she, Mackenzie believed, didn't deserve to be fed or nourished. Mackenzie wished she could be anorexic, strong enough to deny herself sustenance, "courageous" enough to dole out the punishment she believed she deserved for being who she was. Like those who turn to 'pro-ana' websites online, where abstinence from food or bingeing and purging are encouraged, supported, and praised, Mackenzie did not yet recognize that her self-hatred and self-denial only perpetuated the abuse she had received, transforming it into self-abuse.

Yet, despite her previous years of therapy and its ostensibly reparative aftermath, Mackenzie's bulimia had continued unabated. During our first session, she told me that she knew the reason she was bulimic was that her father had molested her. She hated him, she said, and blamed him not only for her bulimia, but for her difficulty in maintaining relationships with men.

As I listened to Mackenzie, I thought about the connection between the sexual abuse she had suffered and her bulimia. Research has shown that a significant percentage of patients with bulimia have experienced such abuse. But what was the direct link between the two? Why was Mackenzie's *particular* response a binge/purge eating disorder, as opposed to some other condition? I knew she had undergone extensive psychotherapy, had acknowledged the abuse and confronted her perpetrator-father. She had worked on the impact the unconscionable boundary violation had had on her self-esteem and her relationships with men. She had even come to accept that the violation had been her father's responsibility and not her own. Yet her struggle with her eating disorder had not abated. Where was the missing link?

Indeed, as we worked together, it became increasingly clear that the seeds for Mackenzie's eating disorder had been sown long before the sexual abuse she had experienced. Mackenzie's rejection by, and longing for, her mother had been with her from the earliest days of her life. Her dependence on the physical feeding for the nurturance she had longed for had manifested in a variety of early gastrointestinal symptoms, and her secret bouts of bingeing went back as far as she could remember. But though she had always longed for a relationship with her mother, her father, it seemed clear, had been her primary source of nurturance. Mackenzie remembered her anticipation of the "special treats" her father prepared for them to share each day after they "played." She recalled, albeit with embarrassment, the feeling of specialness she had felt being the chosen one for his affections. As Mackenzie allowed herself to think about these distressing memories of her life, a painful sense of personal guilt and responsibility began to emerge. She had *liked it*, she tearfully acknowledged. She had loved her father's attention, looked forward to the times they "played" together. It was only later, as she grew older and began to feel that their "little secret" was not right, that she became anxious and tried to tell her mother about it. But by then, her mother hadn't believed her. She had gotten what she deserved, Mackenzie believed. It was all her own fault.

Mackenzie's very existence had garnered the resentment of her mother and siblings, her place in the spotlight of her father's attentions adding fuel to the fiery brew between her parents and leaving her vulnerable to her father's inappropriate actions. Thus, it was not the molestation alone that had driven the dynamics of Mackenzie's eating disorder; it was the entire history of her life. Mackenzie needed to come to terms with the conflicting feelings of longing for the mother she had so desperately needed—and the rage she had felt in response to her mother's verbal and physical abuse and neglect. She needed to confront the sense of guilt she harbored for what she secretly believed to be her own retaliation against and "betrayal" of her mother. At the deepest core of her being, she needed to confront the shame, and understand and forgive herself for being what she believed herself to be: A willing and culpable participant in the tryst with her father.

But most painful of all, Mackenzie needed to come to the realization that, despite all that had happened, despite the estrangement between them, she had loved her father then, and still did. Everyone told her that it was not her fault and encouraged his banishment from her life. Therapist after therapist had tried to re-assure her that it was the parent's responsibility to set the boundaries. But what Mackenzie had been unable to sort out was the incongruity of her life: The father who had treated her kindly, who had always loved her, was the criminal; the mother, whom she felt had always hated her, had taken on the mantle of innocent victim. Unable to make sense of the 'house of lies' in which she had been raised, Mackenzie's hunger for safety, reliability, and untainted acceptance had continued to be physically enacted by way of her eating disorder.

How many people have sat on my couch through the years, expressing their shame for being who they are, their guilt for doing what they perceive themselves to have done? I've heard these stories again and again, often accompanied by tales of self-harm, burning, cutting, and other physical enactments. I've listened to people who have resorted to shoplifting or stealing what they believe they can't get by legitimate means, or to prostitution in a desperate attempt at being held. I've shared the struggle with people who have turned to drugs or alcohol or pornography in search of a few moments of relief—addictive substances and enactments all given up far more easily than their eating disorders, as they are defensive attempts at *leaving* or *losing* the mind, rather than finding it. Mackenzie had been "caught" needing and now she punished herself for needing at all.

Mackenzie's eating disorder was a survival mechanism: It was the way she had been trying to *help*, not *hurt* herself or others, the way she had devised to keep herself functioning in a world that made little sense. Bingeing was a constant and comforting companion, predictable, ever-available, non-judgmental, a balm for her perpetual wounds. Purging was the vehicle by which she attempted to cleanse her shame and her guilt. Could she understand the depth of the neediness and pain she had lived with? Could she forgive herself?

For Mackenzie needed to learn far more than that her parents were wrong, responsible, and should have known better. She needed to learn about her own love; that it was good and worthy of being received; that her needs and desires for closeness and connection had been neither excessive nor toxic. And beyond the knowledge and acknowledgement of the specific abuse and trauma she had lived through, she needed to recognize how she continued to recreate and perpetuate the cycle of abuse by way of her treatment of herself, the way the bonds of shame continued to hold her hostage to a non-nurturing life.

Mackenzie had spent her lifetime feeling unknown and unknowable, and had gone to unimaginable lengths to keep herself from re-experiencing the unbearable pain this had caused her. In her efforts at protecting herself, she had not let anyone in on her secret life. She had not shared her feelings of shame or worthlessness; she had not let on to the uncertainty she felt in relation to herself or others, or her doubts about her own culpability. Living as her own shame-ridden 'toxic container', her sense of alienation and isolation had all been carefully masked. But underneath it all, she was still as frightened and as vulnerable, as deeply affected by her world, as she had been as a little girl—hiding in plain sight of those who could not see her.

Mackenzie had continued reaching out for emotional connection and relief in the feeding, but the food had delivered only half its promise: It had fed her body, but not her mind. While her body had grown more and more full with food, she had still been left hungering for the emotional connection and understanding she yearned for. Identified with the unfiltered toxicity she contained within her, yet unable to 'think' it, share it with others, or otherwise emotionally 'evacuate' it, she had learned to process her experiences alone, with the food—the only thing—she believed she could reliably count on. But this reliance had cost her dearly. For despite all her efforts, she still felt deficient: Never good enough, worthy enough, thin enough, acceptable enough; ashamed for wanting and needing what she believed she couldn't have, shouldn't want, or did not deserve.[1] Mackenzie had spent her life reaching out for the rest of the meal, for the unencumbered emotional connection and nurturance she still unconsciously believed lay hidden in the food. Her body still spoke what her mind could not yet translate into the language of connection.

## Note

1   Kullman, A. (2007). The 'perseverant' personality: A pre-attachment perspective on the etiology and evolution of binge/purge eating disorders. *Psychoanalytic Dialogues*, 17(5): 705–732, 724.

# *foreign relations*

"I TRIED TO CALL YOU over the weekend," Eden began her Tuesday session looking uncomfortable. "I couldn't reach you."

"Oh," I replied, surprised. "I'm sorry I missed your call. I don't *think* I got a message."

"I didn't leave one," she said. "I didn't want to bother you."

"It wouldn't have bothered me," I assured her, knowing well that Eden would not have called if it were not important. Eden had never before called between sessions. 'Reaching me', I felt certain now, had far greater significance than finding me at the other end of the telephone line. "Was everything okay?"

"Josh and I had a fight," she looked down, avoiding my glance. "The worst ever. I've hardly spoken to him since the weekend."

I waited to hear the details, but Eden remained silent for several minutes.

"I've been reading this biography of Princess Diana," she finally said, taking an unexpected turn. "It made me so incredibly sad. She was bulimic, you know."

I nodded, listening carefully for the connection between her difficult weekend and Princess Diana's story.

"She had such a sad life," Eden sighed. "Her mother just abandoned her, and her father was so formal and distant. And then she married Prince Charles, who was in love with another woman! Can you imagine? It's like her whole life, she must have hoped for someone to love her, literally like the fairy-tale—*"someday my prince will come."* And *then*, she finds the prince and ends up just as alone with him as she was with her own family. No wonder she was bingeing and purging and throwing herself down stairwells. It just makes me so sad."

Eden brushed away the lock of hair that had fallen in her face and I noted the cloudy misting in her eyes.

"Do you have any thoughts about why this is affecting you so much right now?" I asked.

"I think I feel so much like her in so many ways," she replied, the sadness in her voice seeming to permeate the room. "Not that we had the same lives, obviously. But just the sadness, the loneliness; feeling like no matter how great your life may appear on the outside, you can still feel alone."

Eden paused again. "I mean, it's not as if I've had such a horrible life," she said, unconsciously straightening her posture—and her story. "My parents didn't abandon *me* or anything. And it's not as if Josh is anything like Prince Charles. I *know*—at least, I *think* I know—that he loves me. I don't think Diana was that fortunate."

I knew that Eden had not been abandoned or abused, but her life had held its own set of challenges. Her father had been in the career military and had served many extended tours of duty overseas. Her mother had "held down the fort" at home, working two jobs and depending on Eden to manage the household and fix meals for her older, drug-dependent brother. Eden's mother had been raised in an abusive home and she was determined that there be peace in hers. She wanted her children to "be happy," she often said, and insisted that any "negative emotions" immediately be abandoned in favor of a "positive outlook on life." And though Eden always looked forward to her father's return, the atmosphere in the home quickly turned with tension when he did. Eden had little experience working things through in her family. She had learned to swallow her feelings, and had spent much of her life physically trying to throw them up.

"Would you like to tell me about your weekend?" I asked, gently.
Eden nodded, and taking a deep breath, thrust her left hand toward me. There was a beautiful, marquis-shaped diamond ring adorning her ring finger.

"Josh asked me to marry him Friday night," she said, glumly.

"Oh!" I replied, startled, not knowing whether to offer congratulations or condolences! Eden had been dating Josh for almost two years, and while their relationship at times had been rocky, she had more than once referred to him as the "love of her life."

"Is that a *good* thing?" I asked tentatively.

Eden flashed a wan smile and nodded, but the shadow in her eyes quickly returned.

"I'm really nervous," she said. "We ended up in this huge fight."

"What were you fighting about?"

"Josh took me to dinner at this little French restaurant," she said, looking down at her ring, carefully examining its glistening facets. "He got down on one knee and pulled out this tiny jewel box—just the way I always dreamed it would be."

"*Some day my prince will come . . .*" I thought, recalling Eden's earlier words.

"But things didn't go so well after that. We started arguing even before we left the restaurant."

"What were you arguing about?"

"Josh wants us to live together," she replied. "He wants us to get a one-bedroom apartment. He thinks we should save money so we can buy a house."

"And what do you think?"

"I think we should get a two-bedroom/two bath." She paused. "But what I *really* think is going on is that I don't feel ready to live together at all."

"I see," I reply. "Any thoughts on what that is about?"

"When you live together, you can't *ever* be alone." Eden's voice took on an unexpected urgency. "Sometimes I feel *relieved* to be alone. And I really *like* being able to leave when I want to. I mean, it's not as if I *don't* want to be with him. When we're not together, I can't wait to see him. But then, when he comes over, I can't wait for him to leave. And when I go over to his place, I constantly think about how I can escape. I can feel totally close to him one minute and then like I don't even know who he is the next. And now that we're engaged . . ." Eden swallowed hard and stared at her ring finger again. "Now that we're engaged, I just feel panicked. I don't know *how* I feel about being together all the time. I don't know how I'll manage."

I understood Eden's dilemma. Much as she had spent her life longing for emotional connection, she had little experience at navigating such connections. When "something happened," when her senses became overwhelmed, her automatic emotional fallback position had always been the solitary, 'one-person' solution represented by her eating disorder. Food had been her most trusted companion, her most intimate relationship, over the course of her lifetime. It had always been there for her, available, with no strings attached—at least no immediately apparent ones. When conflict arose, when her feelings became unmanageable, food had calmed her down, soothed her senses, stood in for the emotional connection she longed for, but hadn't known how to find. I knew that she was genuinely afraid that her only known method of processing her thoughts and feelings would be taken from her and she had no idea how she would manage without it.

Indeed, Eden could see what it looked like to be in a relationship, but had a hard time figuring out how to be truly present in one. Her childhood experiences had not taught her that her emotions were valid or worthy of being addressed. Moreover, the absence of genuine communication in her family had translated into an inability to embrace relationships as a means of shared exchange, comfort, or relief. Unfamiliar with the normal cadence of relatedness—connection, mis- or dis-connection, and repair—any breach in attuned interaction invariably triggered a profound sense of emptiness, loss, and despair for her.[1] Eden's difficulty in understanding how other people thought and felt extended to wondering why they didn't act in ways she expected. She could easily get lost trying to figure out how or why a 'disconnect' had occurred, or whether she 'should' or 'shouldn't' feel as she did. Eden didn't intentionally *break* connections with others; she simply had little idea how to make or maintain such connections.

As I waited for Eden to speak again, a laundry list of possibilities wove its way through my mind: Was her ambivalence related to some specific discomfort with Josh? Had her yearning to finally 'belong' to *someone* clouded her decisions? Were her conflicts related to her difficulty in discerning the 'terms of engagement' of an intimate relationship, the give and take of a 'two-person psychology'? Had she unconsciously gravitated toward a relationship that threatened the distance she had become accustomed to? What were the implications of thoughts she had not allowed herself to think, of conflicts she had not allowed herself to feel?

"What do you think this might be about?" I asked Eden now. "Does it have to do with the way Josh is with you? Is something feeling not quite right—perhaps something you have been afraid to let yourself think or feel about?"

"I don't *think* it has anything to do with Josh in particular," Eden replied, "even though I *was* upset with him all weekend. But even when we're not arguing, it's like I get this tension build-up in me. I can be fine all day, and then suddenly I just want out. Usually I'm okay until we eat. But once we start eating, I can't wait to get away."

Eden paused.

"What if Josh finds out?" she asked anxiously.

"What if he does?"

"It would mean that I couldn't hide anymore."

"Yes, it might mean that you couldn't hide anymore. But then what?" We both sat in silence for several moments.

"You've grown up using food to help you think through your most difficult emotions," I reminded her gently. "And you have come to feel deep shame for having needs you believed were too much for others to bear—even too much for *you* to bear. Chances are you've never shared most of those feelings with *anyone*. Hiding your neediness is the way you've tried to protect yourself."

Eden sighed deeply. "It's not that Josh doesn't know," she said. "I know he knows. It's just that I can't bear to talk about it. Besides you, I don't think there's *anyone* I let in on what's really going on with me."

"It wouldn't surprise me if sometimes it might be a real struggle for you to let *me* in," I nodded my understanding.

Eden looked away. "I guess it does happen with you, too," she said. "Every time I come, I struggle because I don't want to come. But then when I get here, I'm always glad I came. And when I leave, I always wonder why I didn't want to come. But the next time, I don't want to come all over again. And to be honest," she continued, as I nodded my encouragement, "sometimes I act like I'm here, but I'm not really here. I'll tell you a story of something that happened or find some way to fill up the time and the space until our session is over, but I'm not really here, or letting you know what's really going on with me. There's this whole other track going on in my mind that has to do with when I can go to lunch or what I'm going to eat when we're done. That's exactly how it is with Josh, too," she conceded.

I knew that speaking truth to and about her eating disorder was a major developmental achievement for Eden, a key to disabling its grip on her. For much as she hungered for connection, I knew she couldn't just 'wish' her way into counting on me or Josh or anyone to be as consistently available and reliable as food. As long as food served as the 'neutralizer' and secret container for her emotional states, she would remain locked in her insular world, trying to keep herself safe from the unpredictable 'others' who confused and confounded her life. Food held out the promise of relief no living 'object' could consistently provide. Would learning to trust another human being to be as available and reliable as food—or to tolerate the frustrations and delays in gratification required for human interaction—even be possible for her?

"You know," Eden leaned forward. "Food has always been my best friend, but I was always ashamed of needing it. Even when I was a little girl,

I was ashamed. I used to sneak into the kitchen, try not to make any noise, take food I hoped no one would notice was missing. Or I'd let my mother think that my brother ate it. I didn't want anyone to know. I was so ashamed, even then."

"You were ashamed for needing what you thought you couldn't have," I reflected. "Food made you feel better, at least for the few moments before you became ashamed. It wasn't that there was anything *wrong* with what you needed; it was that there was no way to get those needs met. So, you took care of yourself in the only way you knew how. Now, after a lifetime of 'thinking' with your body, that is still what you trust most. You are afraid of losing the only thing you can count on."

Eden dropped back against the sofa and grew silent once again.

"Were you able to tell Josh how or what you were feeling?" I asked her.

"I couldn't," she replied. "I didn't know what to say."

"So, he still doesn't know?"

Eden shook her head. "I'm not even sure I should keep this," she said, twisting the ring on her finger, her voice barely audible. "It's not fair to Josh to say I'll marry him when I'm too scared to even live with him." She hesitated. "But I really do miss him."

"It sounds like underneath the upset, you've felt really scared and alone," I reflected, making the connection between Eden's earlier sadness about Princess Diana and the turmoil of her weekend. "It's especially difficult when you and Josh aren't on the same page. You've been struggling with huge issues in your life—living together, getting married, deciding what to do about your eating disorder—but you haven't been able to share those things with the person closest to you. It seems a little ironic, doesn't it, that just when you need Josh most, you end up shutting him out?"

"I shut *him* out?" Eden sat straight up and stared at me.

"You said you haven't talked to him since the weekend. Is that right?"

"Well, yes," she hesitated. "But that's different."

"How so?"

"He was being so stubborn about the apartment," she said defiantly. "I felt like he wasn't listening to me or taking me seriously. I felt hurt that he treated me so badly and that's why I couldn't talk to him. I didn't *want* to talk to him."

"And then you were *really* left alone," I suggested. "There was just you and the hurt and the food, trying to get rid of the feelings by yourself, trying to purge them out of you."

"So, are you saying that I should *never* get mad at him?" Eden stared at me, and I immediately heard echoes of her mother's directive to "be happy" and avoid "negative emotions" embedded in her question.

"Well, I don't know about that," I replied. "But I wonder whether 'getting mad' or being hurt is a way of disconnecting. I wonder whether it becomes the rationale for holing up inside yourself and reinforcing your belief that you really *are* alone."

Eden took a deep breath. "I didn't know what else to do," she mumbled, once again growing silent.

"You know," she finally said, "my father shuts me out when he gets mad at me. I never thought about it as being the same thing I do with Josh. When it's *me* on the inside, it feels more like I *can't* speak. It doesn't feel like I'm shutting him out or trying to make him feel bad. I just feel . . . well, *mute.*"

"What does 'mute' feel like?" I asked.

"It feels alone," she replied. "Separate. Like there are no words, even if I'd want to say something. But . . . it's strange. Sometimes that 'alone' feeling makes me feel better, stronger, at least for a while. Sometimes I think I even start fights with Josh, just so I can be alone. As much as I feel like I *want* to be close to him, to feel connected, I think I'm so used to feeling alone, it actually feels familiar, even *better* a lot of the time."

"Not dependent on anyone else," I offered. "Not vulnerable to things others might say or do that might hurt you. Feeling comforted with food, alone."

Eden nodded slowly.

"So being empty and alone has really served a purpose," I reflected. "It feels like a relief to not have anything—or *anyone*—inside you. It's the way 'thinking' with your body has helped you through."

"It makes me really sad," Eden stood, as our session drew to a close. "I never realized that when I stop talking to Josh I am leaving *him* alone. He must feel *awful.*"

I nodded my support, and our eyes met for an extra moment as we parted at the door.

★   ★   ★

Committing to marriage is a life-changing prospect for anyone, but for Eden, it represented a monumental challenge. Some perseverant individuals—consciously or unconsciously—gravitate toward relationships that replicate the distance they are accustomed to, choosing partners who allow them to perpetuate their solitary modes of thinking and eating without interruption. Some continue living with a pervasive sense of emptiness and loneliness, counting on food to help them cope even when they are together with others. Eden had tried to control the unpredictable and potentially painful aspects of living by not depending on unreliable others. Her eating disorder had helped her navigate the overwhelming emotional experiences she knew no other way of processing. While her mind had found a solitary solution focused around her fear of 'fat', the true fears underlying her eating disorder—fears of emotional hunger, of psychic emptiness, of taking-in undigestible toxicity, of being alone—had all lain dormant within her.

Now Eden was experimenting with the possibility that making links could bring her nourishment, that emotional connections might be sustainable, that such connections might help her make sense of the chaos in her mind. Much as she was struggling, Eden was beginning the process of shifting her perspective—from hiding her eating disorder to evaluating the role it had played in her life. Difficult as it seemed, she was on the cusp of moving from 'thinking' with her body to thinking with her mind.

## Note

1 Kullman, A. (2007). The 'perseverant' personality: A pre-attachment perspective on the etiology and evolution of binge/purge eating disorders. *Psychoanalytic Dialogues*, 17(5): 705–732, 719.

# Part three

# Thinking with the mind

# *thinking together*

"So NOW THAT JON KNOWS," Megan began her session looking clearly agitated, "he's driving me crazy! He calls me during the day and asks me how I'm doing. The first thing he asks when he walks through the door is, *'So how was your day?'* It's really starting to irritate me!"

"What about it irritates you?" I asked, detecting far more than "irritation" underlying Megan's intense reaction. I knew that her childhood had left her on high alert for hidden messages, meanings, and agendas.

"I feel like its *code*," she bristled. "Like he's *really* asking whether I've binged and purged. Now that he knows, I feel like he's watching everything I put in my mouth. My mother was always worried about whether I was eating 'healthy'—but that was code for whether or not I was on a diet. And my father always wanted to know why I wasn't outside playing sports: *That* was code for him thinking that I looked fat!" Megan paused. "And it's not as if any of it made me eat any *less*. The worse I felt about myself, the more I ate when they weren't around. I just don't want everything to be about what I'm eating or whether or not I've thrown up."

"So, is that the way it feels now with Jon?" I asked. "Like you need to hide or sneak?"

Megan thought again. "No," she said, her voice softening. "It's not the same. I know Jon is trying to be supportive. And when I've had a good day, I really like telling him about it. But when I've had a bad day, when I've struggled or fallen over the edge, I just don't want to talk about it." Megan sighed. "Sometimes I wish he'd just leave me *alone*."

The thing that made getting over her eating disorder so difficult for Megan— or so she thought—was that she couldn't do it alone. She had built her solitary castle in the sky, mastering the art of dealing with her anxiety and conflict without relying on unpredictable others to help manage her distress. Bulimia had protected her from the tensions inherent in relating; it had served as her filter, the way she regulated the flow of what she took in and what she kept out—literally and figuratively. Letting Jon in on her secret world had *seemed* like a good idea at the time, but now she wasn't so sure. There were unspoken messages to decipher, body language to read and interpret, longings and desires he sometimes didn't intuit—not to mention the shame she felt when she was unable to avoid a binge, or when her words or intentions were misinterpreted or misread. It had never occurred to her that *any* form of interacting—even with someone she loved and who loved her—had its own innate stresses. Megan was eager to get over her eating disorder, but couldn't she just do it alone?

Megan had indeed spent much of her life trying to recover from her eating disorder alone. She had read every new book, tried every popular diet, and attempted any number of self-help programs, without sustained success. As a teenager, she had spent a month in an intensive out-patient eating disorder program, learning nutrition and meal planning, participating in group therapy, practicing a variety of cognitive-behavioral strategies to help her intervene in, and/or avoid, a binge. But the program had left her without the insight she needed into the emotional issues underlying her disordered eating and still prone to falling back into its patterns. Group therapy had left her with her "social self" intact, feeling competitive and envious of thinner members, and unable to relate their issues to her own. And while she had accumulated a repertoire of tools for working with her symptoms, she invariably felt defeated when she was unable to sustain her efforts. Time and again she had promised herself to exercise more self-discipline, to control herself, to have more willpower. She made plans to meditate, write in her journal, or just "do better tomorrow." But her reliance on food as her primary mode of thought processing persistently resurfaced, proving too resilient for a short-term, symptom-directed or self-help 'fix'.

Megan couldn't transform a lifetime of thinking with her body by following a scripted protocol, attending a few sessions with a therapist, or tackling the symptoms of her eating disorder on her own. She couldn't suddenly conjure up a new emotional vocabulary or instantly start trusting that others would be there to help contain her anxieties. The scars of her stress-filled childhood would not magically heal, and the cravings and 'food thoughts' that took over her mind would not suddenly disappear because she willed them to. Megan's was still a day-to-day, sometimes moment-to-moment, effort at recognizing, understanding, and tolerating thoughts and feelings she had never before allowed herself to think, feel, or experience. After years of trying to 're-*cover*' (up) her symptoms, she was now steadily working at '*un-covering*' the traumas of a lifetime that had arrested and influenced her development. She was "*dis-covering*" that the solitary way she had tried to manage her distress with food was exactly what had kept her eating disorder intact.

'Un-covery'—what I define as "the achievement of a life-changing under-standing of the underlying dynamics of an addictive or unconscious pattern" —begins with relatedness. For the perseverant individual, learning to think together, to share experiences, to take in regulating input, are the antidotes to the solitary and circular mode of thought processing that characterizes a lifetime of 'thinking' with the body. Contemporary psychoanalytic (or psychodynamic) psychotherapy, in my view, is a living laboratory for easing this shift from body-based to mind-based thinking, from an 'autizoid' 'one-person psychology' to an interactional way of being. In our work together, Megan was discovering a safe space where she could confront her shame-based thoughts and fears, allowing the panic and 'overwhelm' that fueled her use of food for thought to be gently coaxed out of hiding. In the transference, her hopes, fears, expectations, and disappointments were rising to the surface, enacted and examined together, helping her learn to tolerate previously 'unthought' and/or unbearable emotions. Thinking together was helping her 'reboot', recalibrate from reliance on food—an 'inanimate object'—to reliance on living objects who were capable of addressing her hunger for connection in a far more nourishing way.

"Jon wants to come in for a session," Megan said, tentatively. "What do you think?"

I felt instantly enthusiastic at the prospect of Jon joining Megan for a session; transferring the psychotherapy experience from the consulting room into everyday life is the ultimate goal of every therapeutic encounter. Nevertheless, I held back, wondering what the source of Megan's hesitation was.

"What do *you* think?" I asked her.

"I'm not really sure how much I want to share with him," Megan replied. "Jon can be very opinionated, you know! On the other hand, it might be a good thing for him to understand more about what I'm dealing with." She paused. "I feel really ambivalent about it."

Megan had made remarkable strides in the months she had been coming, working hard to make connections between the 'food thoughts' that heralded her binge/purge cycles and her underlying emotional states of mind. She had begun sharing her secret life, first with Jon, and then even inviting her mother to come in for a session. The bonds of secrecy and shame that had characterized her life were beginning to loosen. But thinking alone was still ingrained in her psyche. She still had a hard time reaching out for help when her mind became overwhelmed, often falling back on her tried-and-true method of figuring things out on her own. Thinking together did not come naturally to her, and each step forward had seen its share of struggle.

"How has it been since your Mom came in?" I asked, hoping to help her un-cover the meaning of her hesitation.

"Actually, it's been good," Megan said, looking surprised at the comparison. "There's been a lot less tension between us. She listens to me differently now—like she's really interested in what I have to say, rather than just trying to avoid feeling anything at all."

I was pleased to hear that our joint session with Megan's mother had opened new lines of communication for them. Megan's mother had initially hesitated to come in, fearing that she would be blamed for Megan's eating disorder. But the session had been an eye-opener for both of them—*informational* rather than *confrontational*. We explored Megan's mother's experience of her daughter, hearing *her* perspective on what Megan had been like as an infant and small child. What was it like for her to be Megan's mother? What did each of them see as factors that may have contributed to Megan's eating disorder? The joint session had provided us with the opportunity to observe and learn from the way Megan and her mother related to one another, the kinds of verbal and non-verbal messages they exchanged, the perspective each of them brought to the table in the presence of the other. Megan's mother had listened carefully as Megan shared her experience of her childhood. Both had cried as Megan spoke about the terror she had felt at being left emotionally alone, needing to process her feelings on her own. Mother and daughter had hugged and walked out holding each other. While psycho-analytic psychotherapy has traditionally championed individual sessions, Megan's session with her mother had made an invaluable contribution to our work—and to their lives. Might a session or more with Jon open similar pathways and possibilities?

"Do you think it might be possible," I asked her now, "that when Jon asks you how your day has been he really *is* interested in hearing about it from the 'inside out'? That he genuinely wants to learn about and share in what you are experiencing?"

"Maybe I haven't believed him," Megan was thoughtful. "Or maybe I haven't been able to let it in. I can see that I usually go straight to 'irritated' or 'annoyed' with him. My mind automatically jumps to thinking he means something else."

"That it's 'code'," I echoed her earlier thoughts.

"Yes," she said. "Exactly."

"I wonder, though, whether the *real* 'code' isn't the bingeing and purging," I suggested. "When you've had a hard day and you binge and purge, you have spoken in 'code' with your body. What *really* happened that led you to have the hard day gets lost. When you hide your feelings because you feel confusion or fear or shame, it leaves the code intact: You are still left to process your feelings on your own."

Megan sat silently, thinking for several moments. "You know," she said, "Jon doesn't always get it. Sometimes he says the wrong thing or passes judgment on things I don't really want his opinion on. Those are the times when it gets really hard for me to trust him, no matter how much I want to."

I knew Megan *wanted* to trust Jon. Trust is something we learn early in life—or can struggle with forevermore. Megan still had a hard time remembering that Jon cared about her, even when they disagreed or when he responded to her in a way she didn't expect; mis- or dis-connection and repair were still new concepts for her. But living in connection didn't mean living in a 'warm and fuzzy' state all the time, I pointed out to her. It meant seeing things as they really are, filtering input, dealing with inevitable disappointments, recognizing when she was transferring the expectations or frustrations of her childhood onto Jon or others. Connection also meant considering that others might think differently, but those differences were not necessarily personal affronts. It meant sometimes staying and fighting something through because the relationship was worth the effort.

"I understand that it's hard to trust that Jon will always get it," I said now. "Just when you begin to relax, that infamous 'something' happens that throws you off guard. But the truth is that not Jon, nor I, nor *anyone* can always get things right. In fact, it's not even a matter of *if* or *whether* a glitch in communication or connection will occur, but *when!*"

"I just get so sensitive," Megan nodded slowly. "Just the way my parents used to accuse me of being. I can be fine one minute, and then everything can blow up the next. That's when I shut down and just want to be left alone"

"Short-circuits in connection can also become opportunities," I suggested. "If *I* say or do something that inadvertently hurts you or misses the mark and you let me know about it, we have the opportunity to learn more about what it is like to live inside you—what sorts of things cause a disconnect for you, or cause you distress. If Jon seems critical or distracted or doesn't say the right thing and you let *him* know and give him the opportunity to explain or make things right, the two of you can add another dimension to your intimacy. Recognizing that mis-connections and dis-connections are inevitable parts of relating to others can help *re-connection* become a lot easier to navigate when something goes awry."

"You know," Megan said, "it's ironic. I get mad or withdrawn from Jon because I think *he* is focusing on whether or not I've binged and purged. But the truth is that I'm the one who is making it the issue."

"What do you think the real issue is?"

"Just that I'm struggling," she replied. "I've been having a really hard time. I'm so much better than I was, but I still have days when I fall overboard, when I don't even care what's going on or what the trigger is. I don't *want* to think; I just want to *eat*. I still feel a lot of shame about that. I think I haven't wanted him to know."

Megan shifted positions and looked over at me. "Maybe it *wouldn't* be such a bad idea for him to come in," she smiled sheepishly.

I smiled in agreement. "Maybe!" I said. "Just may be!"

Learning to identify what, when, how, and why her binges were triggered was helping Megan to re-wire her brain and re-frame her expectations. Likewise, learning to *think together* was helping her develop a storehouse of positive inner resources that were beginning to fill the void and replace the emptiness she had tried so long to feed with food. As we considered the kinds of things that overwhelmed her, how the disappointments and expectations of the past had colored her perceptions of the present, their stranglehold on Megan's psyche was gradually diminishing. Megan was finding words where previously there had been none. She was working through the sadness and the mourning for the elusive 'something' she had longed for, but had never been able to find. She was learning that she could survive even the most intense encounters without automatically turning to food to regulate her escalating emotional responses. Megan was building a new repertoire of *relevant* responses to living—how and when and what to do when she felt threatened with 'losing her mind.' Thinking together was challenging the lifelong patterns that had fed her isolation and fueled her eating disorder.

# thinking about thinking

"I'VE BEEN THINKING about thinking," Charlotte picked up on the theme we had been exploring for several weeks. "It suddenly occurred to me to wonder what it even *means* to think! So, I looked it up in the dictionary." She handed me a list and began to read aloud from her own copy:

"To 'think'," she said, "is:

- To have a conscious mind, capable of reasoning, remembering, and making rational decisions
- To employ one's mind rationally in evaluating a given situation
- To have a certain thing as the subject of one's thoughts
- To call something to one's conscious mind
- To consider something as a possible action
- To invent or conceive of something
- To have consideration or regard for someone
- To consider a person or thing as indicated
- To have a belief or opinion
- To have in the mind as an idea
- To evaluate for possible action upon
- To regard as specified
- To believe to be true of someone or something
- To have as a plan
- To anticipate or expect."[1]

"Wow," I exclaimed. "That's quite a list! Does anything in particular jump out at you?"

"I know I'm capable of doing most of those things when my mind is clear," Charlotte replied. "Like when I'm at work or engrossed in a project. I know there are times when I can think really well. But then there are times that I can't do half the things on that list: I can't make a plan or make a decision; I'm not sure what I believe or what my opinions are; I get stressed out over what color nail polish to buy! I must have bought a hundred cans of white paint before I repainted my kitchen, and even then I wasn't sure. Eating is such a relief. It's the only time I don't stress about what I should do. It's like I don't even *want* to think at those times. Sometimes I keep eating so then I won't have to start thinking."

I listened intently to Charlotte's words. "I wonder whether it isn't so much that you don't *want* to think in those moments," I suggested, "but that you don't know *how* or *what* to think. *Something happens*: You hit a wall, lose connection with your mind. You come to a fork in the road, so to speak, and you don't know what else to do—*literally*—but take it!"[2]

Charlotte thought for a moment. "I hadn't thought about it like that," she said. "I've always thought that I eat so I won't *have* to think. It never occurred to me that I eat because I really *can't* think. It's true. It's like I get frozen or stuck, all tangled up in what could happen if I do this or say that. And then, all of a sudden, all I *can* think about is food."

"What are you afraid could happen?"

"Maybe I'm afraid I'll make a mistake," she considered, "and it will be catastrophic. Or maybe it's that I don't know *what* to say or *how* to say it, so I freeze and try to fake it, or act like I know what I'm doing or what I'm talking about when I really don't. And then, I end up not knowing what I think or who I ought to be. I just wish I could be *normal*."

I understood what Charlotte meant when she said she wanted to be "normal." "Normal" for her meant being able to think clearly and concisely, to anticipate consequences. It meant having an inner sense of confidence, guidance, or security, to not struggle. "Normal" people's minds, as Charlotte imagined them, did not spiral out of control or require food to stop the madness. They could *think* about whether it was a good idea to have that piece of cake, or whether it would trigger cravings or make them feel logy or irritable. "Normal" people thought with their minds and not with their bodies.

Charlotte was indeed perfectly capable of thinking when her thoughts did not evoke a disruptive emotional response. Her difficulties arose when an elevated emotional experience caused her conflict, or awakened a particular vulnerability: A clerk at the grocery store was rude or indifferent; her brothers teased her, or friends shared a joke at her expense; a decision needed to be made that she feared might leave her open to criticism or ridicule. Such occurrences could cause her mind to freeze, sending her reeling into "binge-mode," as she called it, racing to food in an effort at regulating her spiraling emotions; racing to help herself continue to think.

"It's like I go from zero to one-hundred in two seconds," she told me. "The minute something gets me off-balance, my mind starts racing and all I can think about is food."

I was encouraged to hear Charlotte grappling with what it meant to think. She had been in therapy for close to a year, and was increasingly "re-*cognize*-ing" the terrors that had dominated her life and the physical ways she had tried to manage them. She was learning how 'thinking' with her body was the way she had tried to process her feelings, exploring ways she had pushed herself to be someone 'better' or 'different' than she was. Charlotte was uncovering deeply rooted doubts that had affected her ability to fully engage in her life, and *dis*-covering that she still often felt too helpless to think about frightening realities.

But, in addition to the insights she was gaining in therapy, it was also clear that Charlotte needed *practical* tools to help her sustain her efforts at keeping track of her mind. She needed to learn what to do with herself when she didn't know what to do with herself, a plan for the times she couldn't remember *why* she had decided not to binge and purge. Like many people who come to see me, Charlotte had previously been in cognitive-behavioral therapy (CBT) for her eating disorder. Many of the strategies she had learned had shared the common goal of helping her slow down the internal freight train in her mind whose destination was a binge. "Take a walk," or "take a bath," "write in a journal," or "recite affirmations"—even sitting in meditation—were all familiar mantras for her. So why couldn't she stick with them, she asked me? Why couldn't she plug one in as needed and keep the train from roaring out of the station, taking her along for the wild ride?

For most veterans of perseverant eating disorders, coping strategies are not enough. They *know* they should be taking that walk, or meditating, or writing in their journals, but the emotions that overtake their minds inevitably require more than modifications for their behaviors. People with perseverant personalities are extraordinarily sensitive and perceptive, deeply affected by the world around them, driven by the persistent 'dyslexithymic' need to know and understand the meaning of their experiences. Many have been accused of being "too sensitive," "too selfish," or "self-absorbed." Many lack the words to express what they feel or the capacity to contain those feelings.

They turn to food in a circuitous and ultimately futile attempt at re-igniting their frozen mental capacities. Nevertheless, their quest is for *meaning*—for comprehension, logic, understanding—the "realizations" that W. R. Bion spoke of—that can transform raw emotion into thoughts that can be used for thinking and tolerating feeling.[3]

Charlotte did not need a generic prescription, or a 'one-size-fits-all' intervention to *distract* her from this quest for meaning. Distractions or interventions can be band-aids, and band-aids are temporary fixes, designed to cover-up unsightly wounds. Uncovering the wound allows the air to flow in and the healing to begin. Charlotte yearned to keep the oxygen flowing, to keep her thinking from short-circuiting. She wanted to be able to stop the train long enough to *think about* what had happened inside her, not distract her. She needed skills that were tailored toward her specific states of mind, and a plan that could be used in conjunction with her therapy to provide her with practical strategies for keeping hold of her mind, organizing her thoughts, and giving herself time to think when escalating emotions threatened to derail her. She needed to build a new repertoire of thinking and feeling *actions and inactions* that could help her learn to tolerate unsettling emotions and situations and challenge her default response of turning to food.

Just as a nurturing parent provides a context or container for the physical, emotional, intellectual, and spiritual needs of a child, so developing a plan for '*un-covery*' that incorporated containing thoughts, patterns, and behaviors was needed to help Charlotte (or any individual with perseverant patterns) build an inner sense of support and security. Treating symptoms alone, without addressing their underlying emotional precursors, ran the risk of leaving Charlotte 're-covering' her symptoms—that is, *covering them up again*—with practical strategies and skills that neither consistently served her, nor broadened her understanding of the emotional dynamics that triggered her enactments. Conversely, uncovering the emotional dynamics of her eating disorder, without simultaneously providing her with a supportive scaffolding of such strategies and skills, could leave her feeling defenseless in the face of emotions that overwhelmed her capacity to think. Taking a 'both/and' perspective, rather than 'either/or', I have come to believe that principles of "the talking cure"—first introduced by Freud, and refined by contemporary relational psychoanalysis—used together with cognitive-behavioral strategies, insight meditation, mindfulness, spirituality, family systems, and so forth—provide a far more cohesive and comprehensive approach to uncovering an eating disorder than any employed on its own. As a perseverant individual learns to identify, define, and tolerate emotional states within the context of the therapeutic alliance, feelings become more tolerable, adjunctive cognitive modalities become more relevant, inner resources begin to develop, and the need to use food for thought correspondingly diminishes.

Together, Charlotte and I explored her options, helping her identify and target cognitive and emotional modalities that would help her sustain her connection to her "thinking" mind. What would help in any given moment, and why? What fears or longings were being stirred up? How could she most directly address or comfort them?

"Let's think about this," I suggested. "Imagine you are beginning to feel nervous or edgy. *Something* has happened but you're not sure what it is. You can *feel* the "emotional storm"[4] brewing in your mind, the tension building in your body, the thoughts of food beginning to take hold. You are on the brink of a binge. Where are the feelings coming from? What are they about? What will help you while you are figuring it out?"

Together we re-considered the many cognitive tools she had already learned, with the renewed goal of personalizing them and making them more relevant to her everyday life and experiences. Some were familiar and *pro-active*, most helpful when practiced regularly, providing a 'frame' for her to count on to help regulate her states of mind:

- *Planning and scheduling*—sometimes in small increments, and/or *making lists* as a way of providing sequencing and structure for chaotic thoughts; a means of containing and organizing the mind, learning to slow down and allow herself to think and focus
- *Writing and/or journaling*—to help translate and give chaotic and/or per-severative thoughts 'concrete' form: A thought-based alternative to purging toxic feelings
- *Reading*—as a means of taking in new thoughts and ideas and exploring their resonance, as well as offering a pleasurable respite
- *Finding 'words to say it'*—working with a list of emotion words (see Chapter 15) to help identify, nuance, and provide context for confusing states of mind
- *Mindfulness*—a state of heightened awareness—with particular emphasis on becoming aware of 'food thoughts' as signifiers of emotional distress
- *Visualization and empathic identification with others*—as a means of developing an 'observing ego' and compassion toward oneself
- *Prayer*—and/or other preferred means of spiritual centering.

Other interventions were aimed at helping Charlotte *de-activate*, that is, engage in activities that promoted peace, relaxation, and a turn-away from the *drivenness* that characterized her intense efforts at "figuring things out:"

- *Listening to music, painting, and/or engaging in other creative arts*—sources of rest and relaxation, connecting body, soul, mind, and spirit, providing soothing, nurturance, and grounding for spiraling emotions
- *Resting*—taking naps or going to bed early—an aid to slowing down and re-centering her body and mind; an opportunity for rejuvenation many perseverant individuals do not afford themselves
- *Meditation*—a boundless wellspring of peace and regulation, helping to calm and soothe the senses, release tension, strengthen the ability to observe, track, and tolerate actions and reactions, and link the physical to the emotional
- *Mindfulness in motion*—engaging in gentle movement, such as stretching, yoga, tai chi, or dance that enhance the connection between body and mind
- *Floating*—swimming, bubble-bathing, resting on a raft or hammock, recreating a sense of being rocked or held
- *Doing nothing*—allowing herself to just 'be'—lay on the grass, stare at the moon, engage in actions that require no *re*-actions.

Such modalities are often encouraged within the context of 'self-help', but self-help, I would argue, is the polar opposite of what the perseverant individual—whose entire psyche is organized around thinking by and for herself—actually needs. As Charlotte and I looked at her options together, I encouraged her to visualize or imagine that she had a friend or a child of her own who was feeling just as she was at any given moment. How would she help him/her cope or gain perspective? Could she treat herself as kindly and gently as she would someone she cared about? As we experimented with applying interventions specifically to her states of mind, Charlotte began to notice that she often binged when she was tired. She could see how refreshed she felt and how much easier it was for her to keep track of her mind after even a short nap. She noted how "luxurious" she felt after a bath, how "grounded" after a walk, how much pleasure she gained from reading a novel after years of immersion in her school books. Charlotte signed up for her first ballet class and took herself out to the movies. It was really different, she told me, to do these things because they *felt* good, because they *helped* her, rather than as *distractions* aimed at forestalling a binge.

Meditation was particularly helpful for Charlotte. For the perseverant who lives with chaos, who is constantly threatened with 'losing her mind', learning to meditate can be transformational. Insight meditation forms a unique psychic partnership with psychotherapy, teaching that the body is an amazing barometer of emotional states. Every emotional reaction has a corresponding physical reaction, causing tension to arise in one or more areas of the body. Making the connection between the physical and the emotional is key to body and mind working together, interactively rather than interchangeably. Charlotte, for example, observed that an instantaneous reaction would often catapult her back to the past or into the future, leaving her disconnected from the present moment and unable to engage her mind to help her sort out the intensity of her experience. By learning to bring her thoughts back to the present moment, becoming aware in intricate detail of what was happening inside her body and mind, Charlotte discovered that she was capable of surviving her own emotional states; that all things, both physical and emotional, arise and pass away. As Charlotte's ability to tolerate and regulate overstimulating physical and emotional experiences strengthened, she discovered a growing sense of peace, groundedness, and an increased ability to *think* before reacting.

Gradually, Charlotte was making tangible connections between bingeing and purging and her difficulty in engaging her mind when she couldn't think or didn't know what else to do with herself. She could see how difficult transitions and unstructured time were for her, how much extra attention she needed to pay to herself when she felt lonely or uncontained. She was absorbing the heretofore 'alien' concept that she needed to be kinder, gentler, and more tolerant of herself, especially when she felt most vulnerable. Slowing down and giving her mind a chance to kick in, Charlotte was dis-covering the kinds of experiences and activities that brought far more soothing and nurturance to her than food had ever provided. The cognitive tools she was employing were making a new kind of sense to her, as she was incorporating new ways of being to replace the hours she had spent in the fog of bingeing and purging.

Each time Charlotte recognized a 'food thought' and made the connection with whatever was happening inside her, she was initiating changes in her brain, laying down new pathways for thinking. Each time she was able to make a mind-based decision about what to do instead of eating, she was strengthening her inner resources and making it less likely that she would need to use food for thought. Charlotte's body and mind were beginning to work together, interactively rather than interchangeably. "Thinking about thinking" was not only helping her un-cover her eating disorder, but helping to transform her mental and emotional *perseveration* into determined *perseverance* to live a conscious, considered, and deliberate life.

## Notes

1   *Random House Webster's College Dictionary* (1992). New York: Random House, p. 1387.
2   This metaphor or joke is of course not original to this case; to the best of my knowledge it can be traced back at least to Berra, Y. (1998). *The Yogi Book: I Really Didn't Say Everything I Said!* New York: Workman Publishing, p. 48. My point in repositioning his quip into a therapeutic context is to underline the therapeutic potential of attention paid to revealing metaphors.
3   Bion, W. R. (1962b). Learning from experience. In *Seven Servants: Four Works by Wilfred R. Bion*, Northvale, NJ: Jason Aronson, 1977, p. 113.
4   Eigen, M. (2005). *Emotional Storm*. Middletown, CT: Wesleyan University Press.

# *thinking about feeling*

WHEN I WAS A YOUNG THERAPIST, barely out of graduate school, a local nursery school asked me to present an evening program for parents, geared toward helping them better understand their children. The past lives on in us, I began. What was life like for *you* as a child? How might *your* experiences still be playing a role in your interactions with your own children? As one parent after another raised their hands, the room came alive with memories, recollections, recognition of ways their own early experiences and traumas might still inadvertently be being transmitted onto their own children.

Suddenly an angry voice, laden with sarcasm, called out from the back of the room. "Don't you think it's time you grew up?" the man demanded. "The past is the past. It's over. Why don't you just *grow up* and move on."

The room froze. The freedom to think, experiment, try on new ideas, acknowledge old ones—all suspended. It took a few moments for equilibrium to be restored, for the group to pick up where they had left off, albeit a bit more cautiously.

What is it about the past that is so unsettling for some? Often it is fear—fear of awakening old memories, of reliving experiences that are too painful or too overwhelming to bear. Fear sometimes grows a crusty exterior on its way to protecting a vulnerable self. *Grow up, move on. Don't take yourself too seriously. The past is the past. You can't change it anyway. Don't think about it. Don't think.*

Sufferers of eating disorders are often raised with such implicit and explicit messages. Becoming heirs to their parents' projected, denied, or disavowed emotions, they are the children who see what their parents would rather not have seen, who react to what their parents would prefer to have swept under the rug. Often such children are accused of being "too sensitive" or "too selfish," labels that cleave to their psyches like barnacles, coating their senses of themselves with shame for having feelings they imagine they shouldn't have, for having needs best kept hidden. *Get over yourself. Don't be so self-absorbed. Forget the past. Just focus on the* pasta.

Psychoanalyst D.W. Winnicott wrote of the "fear of breakdown."[1] What we fear most, he said, is that which has already happened to us. As an infant, the perseverant individual may already have survived a catastrophic sense of aloneness, abandonment, terror, or variations thereof. The memories remain embedded in the unconscious mind, in implicit memories stored in the body, ever-primed for re-awakening in the face of yet another potentially dysregulating emotional event. Feelings associated with disaster—and food, its early antidote—become the automatic 'go-to' mechanism to calm the terror of the moment. Food alone, the perseverant has come to believe, can stave off the disaster and quell the fear of returning to that state of helpless breakdown.

"It's like my whole life is a façade," Ella tearfully told me, "an appearance I try to create. I go through the motions, but really at those times, all I'm thinking about is food and how and when and what I can eat. If people knew the truth about what I really think about half the time, they'd probably be in shock."

"What would they know if they knew what you think?" I asked her.

Ella thought for a moment. "That when I'm hungry, I feel terrified. That if I can't get food, I feel terrified. That when I'm full I feel terrified. That the whole time I'm eating, I'm terrified!"

"Keyword: 'Terrified'," I reflected, nodding. "Bingeing is all about fear. You binge and purge because you are afraid to be empty, afraid to be full, afraid to be alone. But mostly, you are afraid to be afraid. You are afraid you can't or won't be able to tolerate the feeling."

Ella was silent for several moments, her face registering the impact of allowing herself to experience, if only for a moment, the reality of her fear. "I don't know what else to do about it but eat," she said.

Fear is not a character flaw or a failing, I told her. It is more a fragility, a wounding, slow to heal, requiring salve. Histories of abuse or neglect—intended or otherwise—carry inevitable emotional consequences: Shame, guilt, shattered loyalties, fear of causing grief to others, the belief that one has brought things on oneself; the terror of existing alone in the universe.

These are all powerful emotional states that fuel the terror, that give rise to the emotional and physical state of combustion that *is* an eating disorder. When food and thought, body and mind, are inextricably linked, feelings present a unique challenge. Physical hunger may evoke panic, the emptiness (consciously or unconsciously) re-activating the fear for survival, the terror of being left without the critical containment—even if only physical—once embodied by the feeding mother in infancy. Conversely, the sensation of fullness may set off alarm bells, triggering fear of the "toxic containment" experienced as dangerous to the survival of the self. Fears of hunger, of emptiness, of fullness, of being or feeling 'fat' can all be linked to corresponding fears for survival, fears of abandonment, of containing toxic emotions, of needing what others cannot, will not, or are unable to provide. While bingeing momentarily de-escalates the sensation of panic, the perseverant individual is in a perpetual state of what W. R. Bion called "nameless dread."[2]

Uncovering that dread can be a terrifying prospect. The eating disorder serves as a makeshift solution and protective mechanism, and initiating the process of 'un-covery'—*literally* the process of changing one's mind—can be fraught with even more fear, resistance, and self-protective measures. Ella was as convinced as anyone with a perseverant eating disorder that she wanted to be free of bulimia's grip—until the fear returned, until she suddenly felt hungry, frightened, conflicted, or besieged by emotions for which she had no words. The path toward 'un-covery' needed to be a gentle and forgiving one, I told her. People with perseverant personalities invariably believe that they need to be *harder* on themselves, when in truth they need to be kinder and gentler, more patient and compassionate with themselves. Living without food for thought is to swim in unchartered waters. Better not try it *alone* at home!

★   ★   ★

Kendall, too, was afraid to feel. For many months after she began seeing me, Kendall worried that she was a failure every time she succumbed to a binge. A 'good' day would be one in which she managed to keep herself from bingeing or purging; a 'bad' one in which she "lost it," leaving her in despair. Listening to her on one particularly dark day for her, it occurred to me that while Kendall had an impressive vocabulary and was able to articulate many painful and despairing feelings, I could not *feel* them in her. Describing this vague sense to her—that it was as if she was *reporting* her feelings, but was not actually *in* them—what I think of as 'dyslexithymia'—Kendall looked at me with surprise. She knew exactly what I meant, she said. In fact, she had long ago decided to keep herself removed from her feelings because she knew how "awful and damaging" they could be when they did come out.

Kendall associated to a fight she had had with her brother several years before. She had walked in on him making-out with his girlfriend in the family room, and according to Kendall, he had "gone ballistic." He started screaming, "*Get the hell out of here! I'm going to kill you if you don't get the hell out of here!*" Kendall was overtaken by "feelings." She ran to her parents' bedroom, grabbed the handgun out of her father's nightstand, and returning to the family room, screamed at her brother over and over again, "*Here, take the gun! Kill me! Go ahead! Kill me!*" Never before, she said, had she realized how "horrible," "uncontrollable," and "destructive" her feelings could be. She cried for three days after the incident, and resolved never again to express her feelings, but rather to work in every way she could to be a "better" and "different" person.

As we processed her experience, I was struck not only by the literalness of Kendall's interpretation of her brother's words, but also how it had tainted her perception of herself. I pointed out to her that she had not tried to harm her brother, but had demanded to be killed herself. In the moment of greatest intensity, she had no wish to destroy the other, but rather wanted *her own* perceived toxic essence to be eradicated. Never before had it occurred to Kendall that there was a difference between *having* horrible feelings and *being* a horrible, destructive person. This realization brought the first tears Kendall had shed in her analytic sessions—and her first glimmer of hope that it was possible to *feel* and still survive.

Ella and Kendall both entered psychoanalysis, attending sessions three or four times a week, immersing themselves in the process of thinking together with me and tracking their emotional states. Our work was organized around exploring the dynamics of relationships, finding words to capture and describe their thoughts and feelings, and making links between their emotional histories and the physical dynamics of their eating disorders. As we worked together in frequent encounters, historical transference dynamics were able to emerge, thoughts were better able to be tolerated in their minds, and the need to enact their emotional states by way of their eating disorders concurrently diminished. Thinking and feeling about what frightened them in the past helped Ella and Kendall to stop abusing themselves in response to having been abused. In a sense, they were learning to "change the past" by re-evaluating their understanding and perception of it, by allowing themselves to think about it and feel its impact within a containing space.

★ ★ ★

Lucie, an eighteen-year-old college student, had been bulimic since she was twelve years old. When she first came to see me, she told me that she had been "recovered" for six months, yet her perception of herself had never been worse. Lucie hated herself and hated her body, and seemed to be inching back to her eating disorder with every passing binge. As we explored what her life had been like without her bulimia, we discovered that even though she had made radical changes to her eating, her life had still remained very much the same. Her mother still criticized her every move and seemed to be endlessly disappointed in her. Though Lucie would "stand up for herself," argue and fight back, she invariably absorbed and turned every harsh word uttered by her mother back against herself. No matter what she did, she told me, she could not seem to gain her mother's love or approval.

Lucie could not comprehend what it was about her that made her so unappealing to her mother. It would take many months for her to integrate the notion that her mother's projections into and onto her had had little to do with *her*, with whom or how she was. Rather, she was carrying the burden of her mother's own discontent, and no matter how hard she tried, it would not be possible for her to succeed at being a better mother to her mother than her mother's *own* mother had been for *her*. Lucie had taken in her mother's projections and turned them against herself. She carried them around like an albatross around her neck, the crushing self-criticism coloring everything she thought and did. Her toxic self-perception reflected the 'undigestible' feelings she could barely contain on her own.

Writing helped Lucie. Writing and/or keeping a journal are often employed as CBT strategies, with the aim of helping individuals calm, focus, and intervene in the chaotic state of mind before it leads to an eating disorder enactment. But the feelings evoked by writing can also be disruptive and frightening for perseverant individuals, leaving them alone with emotions they don't know how to contain on their own. Though Lucie had tried keeping a journal, it was agonizing for her, stirring up the very emotions her eating disorder had unconsciously conspired to protect her from. *Writing together* during sessions, however, helped mitigate Lucie's trauma, even as it cracked open a window to her unconscious mind. Writing together was a way of protecting her fragile self, offering a hand to hold on the way to learning to think with her mind. It provided Lucie with a containing framework that helped her plumb the depths of her eating disorder:

*I remember growing up and always feeling like my mother hated me. I remember never being able to eat naturally in front of other people, always trying to pretend to be daintier than I really was so maybe my mother would like me better. I remember always wanting so much more than I ever could have. I remember never being full, never feeling like I'd had enough, but knowing I either wouldn't be allowed to have more or being too embarrassed to ask for more and taking the risk that I'd be made fun of. The only way I could get more was by sneaking it. And the punishment for sneaking it was my mother's anger and getting fat and being teased and taunted for being fat. Sneaking into the refrigerator on Sunday afternoons when people were sleeping after dinner. Sneaking whenever I could manage to do it and no one was around. Wanting, wanting, wanting so much more than I could ever in a million years find, and then covering it up. I remember the hunger. When I was good, I was starving. The only way I could be good was if I was on a diet and starving. I got love for starving. Now I'm still starving, even when I eat. I've been starving all my life. Now that I'm old enough to decide for myself and no one else can force me to starve, I have to eat. I have to sneak. I have to eat whatever I can because if I don't it won't be there anymore. I might miss something and I can't stand to miss anything else anymore. Food is my best friend because food is the only thing that understands how starving I am. Food is the only thing that knows how to give me what I need. I have to have food because I don't have anything else. I don't have anyone or anything else that understands. I don't know what else to do.*

Plumbing the depths of her painful feelings made it possible for Lucie to acknowledge and pay attention to them. Rather than swallowing her pain, writing together helped her begin to share her inner world for the first time in her life—and allowed me to serve as a 'container' for her toxic emotions.

★    ★    ★

My patient Mia had a different challenge when it came to feelings. Mia had a limited emotional vocabulary, invariably relegating her experiences to the categories of "mad, glad, or sad." She, too, had missed out on connecting with feelings, on learning to use the *nuances* of language to help her flesh out the scope of her experiences. Mia didn't have the words to describe the unformulated chaos within her; she couldn't let herself know *how*, or even *that*, experiences affected her, that *something* was making her afraid. She couldn't tolerate the pain of disappointment or humiliation—or even the over-stimulation of being excited. Lacking words to express her intentions, Mia's mind skipped over pain or anxiety—or assigned words that reflected her confusion: She was "thrilled" and "ecstatic" to be feeling so badly, she told me one day—and it was only upon parsing her meaning that we discovered the relief she felt at feeling *something* other than the craving and insistent 'food thoughts' that normally dominated her mind. Mia literally lacked the tools for *thinking about feelings*.

Mia was aided by working directly with words. Providing her with a list of emotions (see Table 1), we worked together during sessions to find words and language that could capture and communicate her intent, provide form and substance for her thoughts and feelings, and forge a pathway from the unthinkable to the conceivable. Finding words helped Mia transform feelings from harbingers of disaster to signals that something needed to be paid attention to or be addressed. Creating language that conceptualized experience—new words that invited new thoughts and new ways of identifying nuances—began expanding her tolerance for emotional stimulation that had been short-circuited by her binge/purge enactments.

Spending my life as I do, listening to patients like Ella and Kendall, Lucie and Mia, I find that it has become virtually impossible for me to take in language at face value. A patient will use words like "mad, glad, or sad," or a student will use words like "borderline," "enactment," "fragmentation," "disintegration" or "annihilation," and my brain grinds to a halt. *What exactly do they mean?* Similarly, words like "frustrated" or "irritated" can't tell us much about the specifics of the speaker's state of mind. These are generic words, words that sound like they have standardized or universal meanings, but in reality, are unique to each individual experiencing them. What is the emotional experience they are trying to convey? What does the word or experience feel like, remind them of, sound like in their minds, feel like in their bodies? Are they saying what they indeed *feel*, or using words to avoid the secrets they are ashamed of or feeling too vulnerable to reveal? It is as if my own mind becomes intentionally 'dyslexithymic', insisting that every syllable or nuance be allowed to declare its rightful position in the construction of *the experience of the experience*.

Without a reliable way of formulating experiences in words, the mind freezes over and perseveration ensues. Food, and the rhythmic re-creation of the feeding, emerge as a means of organizing the chaos in a mind that

*Table 1*  A (sample) List of Emotions[3]

| | | | |
|---|---|---|---|
| Happy | Anxious | Ashamed | Fuming |
| Contented | Longing | Useless | Stubborn |
| Relaxed | Desirous | Worthless | Belligerent |
| Calm | Dreading | Ill at ease | Confused |
| Satisfied | Sorrowful | Weepy | Awkward |
| Comfortable | Sad | Vacant | Bewildered |
| Peaceful | Unhappy | Hurt | Fearless |
| Joyous | Depressed | Injured | Encouraged |
| Ecstatic | Melancholy | Isolated | Courageous |
| Enthusiastic | Gloomy | Offended | Confident |
| Inspired | Somber | Distressed | Secure |
| Glad | Dismal | Pained | Independent |
| Pleased | Quiet | Suffering | Reassured |
| Grateful | Mournful | Worried | Bold |
| Cheerful | Dreadful | Crushed | Brave |
| Excited | Dreary | Heartbroken | Daring |
| Lighthearted | Flat | Cold | Strong |
| Carefree | Dull | Upset | Determined |
| Surprised | Moody | Lonely | Loyal |
| Optimistic | Sulky | Despairing | Proud |
| Exhilarated | Low | Tortured | Impulsive |
| Playful | Discouraged | Angry | Interested |
| Elated | Disappointed | Resentful | Concerned |
| Thrilled | Concerned | Irritated | Fascinated |
| Silly | Unsympathetic | Enraged | Engrossed |
| Eager | Choked up | Furious | Intrigued |
| Compassionate | Embarrassed | Annoyed | Absorbed |
| Curious | Humiliated | Set-up | Doubtful |
| Creative | Afraid | Outraged | Skeptical |
| Sincere | Fearful | Vengeful | Distrustful |
| Sympathetic | Pathetic | Bitter | Suspicious |
| | Belittled | Grumpy | Uncertain |

does not have the words to identify, contain, or give meaning to thoughts that cannot be used for "thinking, dreaming, or making links"[4] with others. Food remains the physical representation of thought. Resting in the knowledge that feelings and thoughts can be 'held'—not only in the minds of others, but in the *words* that those feelings are entrusted to—helps unravel the chaos and un-cover the thinking mind.

## Notes

1   Winnicott, D. W. (1974). Fear of breakdown and the unlived life. *International Review of Psychoanalysis*, 1: 103–107.
2   Bion, W. R. (1962a). A theory of thinking. In *Second Thoughts: Selected Papers on Psychoanalysis*. Northvale, NJ: Jason Aronson, 1967, p. 116.
3   Adapted from a variety of internet sources and personal additions, 2016.
4   Bion, W. R. (1959). Attacks on linking. In *Second Thoughts: Selected Papers on Psychoanalysis*. Northvale, NJ: Jason Aronson, 1967, pp. 110–119, 105.

# *thinking about eating*

"CAN WE JUST TALK ABOUT FOOD today?" Kaitlin began her session.

"Of course," I replied, my psychic radar instantly deploying. Just as 'food thoughts' serve as 'red flags' for as yet unformulated experiences that are causing distress, so "just talking about food" could be Kaitlin's way of letting me know that something distressing was going on in her mind. Food is so integrally intertwined with thinking for people with perseverant eating disorders, that it is an inevitable and frequent area of discussion for us. But what specifically was stirring Kaitlin today?

"I'm still having such a hard time," she persisted. "I keep trying to eat healthy and I do fine most of the day. But then, by the afternoon, it just starts building and before I know it, I *have* to eat. When it hits me like that, it's all I care about."

"What starts building?"

"A whole lot of things," she replied. "Sometimes it's tension at work, or not knowing what to do with myself if I'm home alone. My body starts feeling this empty feeling; my mouth starts feeling this *gnawing*. And it grows and grows until it's the only thing I can think about."

"Well, let's talk about the physical part of this, then, for a minute," I suggested. "You say you try to 'eat healthy'. What does 'eating healthy' mean?"

"It means eating fruits and vegetables, salads," Kaitlin said. "No refined carbs. No gluten. No dairy. No fat. Just a little bit of protein."

"And how does that sound to you now, even as you say it?"

"It doesn't sound *bad*," she replied. "I really *like* eating salads and fruits and vegetables. I feel good inside when I eat that way."

"It sounds like you are talking about *more* than the way your body feels, though," I reflected. "Almost like what you eat has the power to make *you* a 'good' or 'bad' person."

"It's just that I'm so frustrated!" Kaitlin said, sidestepping my analogy. "I keep trying to eat right. I keep trying to listen to my body and only eat when I'm hungry and stop when I'm full, but it doesn't work. I can't sustain it. I always end up bingeing and then I have to purge."

"Well, I think we know that every time that happens, *something* has happened to upset the balance for you. But I'm also wondering whether 'trying to eat healthy' may be part of the problem."

"What do you mean?" Kaitlin eyed me suspiciously. "You don't think I *shouldn't* eat healthy, do you?"

"Well, *theoretically*, I don't think that," I replied. "But when you're dealing with un-covering an eating disorder, trying to 'eat healthy' can sometimes become a trap. For one thing, cutting out carbs and limiting protein is putting enormous stress on your body and is undoubtedly contributing to your hunger, cravings, and other physical stressors—not to mention compromising your long-term health. From an emotional perspective, you promise yourself to 'be good': You'll eat your vegetables, or count your calories, or carbs, or fats. But the reality is that your relationship with food is multi-layered; it's not just about maintaining your health. When you've lived with food substituting for care and comfort, food to help you think, food to help you survive emotionally, the remedy can't just be to expect yourself to eat perfectly or 'healthfully' all the time. *All* the elements affecting your body *and* your mind need to be taken into account."

"So, what am I missing?"

"Well, I wonder whether 'eating healthy' might be what some people call 'code' for telling yourself that certain foods are off-limits. Perhaps you tell yourself that to be 'good' you can never again eat pizza or pasta or chocolate; perhaps you think it means that you will forever be deprived. Deprivation is the mother's milk of a binge! If you are trying to eat in accordance with some outside rules, rather than in response to sensations and decisions coming from inside of you, you may be setting yourself up for a binge."

What exactly did 'eating healthy' mean then, Kaitlin and I explored. In our 'one- size-fits-all' culture, it can be easy to assume that there is an ideal way, a single perfect plan that, if followed precisely, can lead to universal reconciliation of food and eating disturbances. But the reality is that some people thrive on animal proteins and others on plant-based diets; some can tolerate glutens, and others expand exponentially with every grain in a rice bowl. Much as Kaitlin yearned for a definitive answer, there were no hard and fast rules I or anyone could provide her. Getting to know her own body and its responses by way of our work together, and engaging her mind in decision-making about what she took in and what she didn't, was her best hope for separating out eating disorder 'directives' from genuine signals being sent by her body. But avoiding fats, carbs, gluten, dairy, or proteins because of fear that they were inherently dangerous or would cause her to become toxically 'fat', was more akin to what is called "orthorexia"[1]—a form of obsessive food restriction and eating disturbance that masquerades as 'eating healthy'. For people with perseverant eating disorders, such limited, deprivation-based forms of eating are one-way tickets to ongoing binge/purge eating disorders.

"Having that piece of chocolate is not what leads to a binge," I point out to Kaitlin. "It is the *'OMG-I-just-had-a-piece-of-chocolate-and-now-it's-all-over-and-I-have-to-keep-eating-so-I-can-throw-up'* that keeps you caught in the 'closed-circuit loop' of your eating disorder."

*'Thinking* about eating' means slowing down the mind and considering options. The surges of emotion that repeatedly sent Kaitlin reeling toward a binge had also left her unfamiliar with the process of decision-making that is an integral part of thinking. Kaitlin wasn't used to *deciding* whether to eat that first chip, or piece of bread, and/or deciding when to stop. She had little experience with *choosing* to have just a spoonful or two of dessert, if that was what she really wanted, or paying attention to whether or not she still wanted the dessert after that first bite. On the other hand, *not* eating a particular food because she genuinely disliked it, or because it caused her gastric distress, were examples of *thinking* decisions based on her own physical proclivities. Kaitlin was the expert on her own body and mind, and focusing on what she knew about her own needs was a critical step in helping her transition from thinking *with her body* to *thinking about eating* with her mind.

While I could not determine *for* Kaitlin what was best or "healthy" to eat, we *could* explore and consider her options together:

- Did she do best with planned meals, with eating what she wanted when she was hungry, with choosing from a list of 'safe' foods?
- Did she do well with high-protein, low-fat, high-carb grain-based diets, or a combination of all of the above?
- Did she do better eating at home, or eating out?
- Did she feel more focused eating alone, or with others?
- Did she prefer to plan for specific meals, or 'graze' when she felt hungry?
- Did she generally favor hot or cold foods?
- Was any particular meal particularly important to her?

- Was any meal more difficult than others?
- Would being 'flexible' in her selections create too much anxiety?
- Would pre-set selections make her feel deprived?
- How important were the 'atmospherics' surrounding eating for her?

As we explored Kaitlin's likes and dislikes and how they related to her relationship with food, more deeply embedded thoughts and fears emerged: How much more vulnerable she felt in some places, and with some people, than with others; how afraid she was of finding herself in less-than-ideal circumstances; how worried she was of losing focus. We considered various possibilities: How might she help someone else out of a similar dilemma? What might her options be in any given situation? Giving her fears 'concrete' form and substance began helping Kaitlin develop her ability to observe— to gain distance and perspective—and prepare her for thinking about eating even in unexpected or dysregulating situations.

Whichever eating plan Kaitlin ultimately decided upon, I knew it would inevitably get difficult. Despite her belief that her struggle was with food, her bulimia had far less to do with the food she consumed than with the disorienting directives in her mind—the perseverant thinking that compelled her to feed her distress with food instead of with thought. When she found herself craving food when she wasn't physically hungry, it was not just her body speaking to her; it was her anxious, terrified, and vulnerable mind calling on her body to protect her. At her core, Kaitlin feared that losing access to food threatened her survival. She feared that she would be unable to make it through the day, or the week, or the rest of her life without her primary mode of processing her thoughts and feelings—the food she had come to believe made it possible for her to think.

"I know that dieting or restricting doesn't work," Kaitlin told me. "But I think I do it anyway. I tell myself I can only eat certain things, and by the afternoon I'm so hungry, I'll start craving carbs or fats. Telling myself that it would be bad to eat them takes up only about ten seconds," she said. "Then I tell myself I can throw up 'just this one more time'."

Kaitlin was silent for several minutes. "Anytime there's something inside of me, I feel like I'm *bad*," she said. "I shouldn't have anything inside me. I shouldn't *eat*. Every time I eat, I feel like I've lost the battle. God, I wish I could be anorexic! I wish I could be strong enough to *never* eat, but I'm *not*. I keep *needing* to eat and I keep failing."

"It sounds like right now, there isn't much difference in your mind between food and feelings," I observed. "Food inside you doesn't feel any different than the feelings that are *really* making you feel bad. An anorexic tries to keep herself safe by keeping food *out*. She's afraid that if she takes in anything at all—food *or* feelings—it will kill her. The sad irony is that, far too often, her refusal to take in *does*." [2]

"I know," Kaitlin said glumly. "When I'm in my right mind, I know that what *looks* strong is really suicidal."

As Kaitlin fell into a long silence, I found myself thinking how often I had heard patients with cyclical binge/purge eating disorders express a similar wish to be anorexic. Some people with perseverant eating disorders are mistakenly referred to as 'purging anorexics'—a significant misnomer, in my view, as individuals who suffer severe emaciation due to multiple purging episodes do not suffer from a 'lack of appetite'. On the contrary, their hunger and need is so great, they can barely refrain from feeding it; nor can they tolerate the presence of what they perceive to be toxic inside their bodies for more than moments at a time. The severely emaciated individual who binges and purges, in fact, may well stand at the most perilous end of the perseverant spectrum, as susceptible to losing her battle with life as is her anorexic sister.

On the other hand, individuals who suffer from what I call 'restrictor' eating disorders—including anorexia nervosa, chronic obesity, and chronic starvation dieting—present with very different psychodynamic profiles than their perseverant siblings. Where the psyche of the perseverant is organized around a longing *to take in*, the psyche of the restrictor is organized around the attempt at *keeping out*. Empirically we know that anorexics have developed the capacity to *wait*, to delay the feeding indefinitely. This capacity to delay gratification is a developmental milestone not normally achievable until the second year of life. It implies that a secure attachment was once established—allowing for the development of such milestones—but was later lost. The mother's care, for example, which may have been perfectly attuned to the developmental needs of her *newborn*, may become overly-intrusive or controlling for her older infant or individuating toddler (or later teen). Research, in fact, has shown that while mothers of bulimics tend to be *under*-involved with their children, mothers of restricting anorexics tend to be *overly*-involved and/or intrusive with theirs. [3] The resistance to the mother's control may then be played out on the battlefield of this child's body over what she will or will not take in

"My mother won't ever leave me alone," fifteen year old Stephanie sobbed. "She monitors everything I eat. She reads my journal and scrolls through my text messages and calls my friends and their parents and asks them about me." Arguing that she "just didn't like" what her mother cooked," Stephanie's anorexia expressed her symbolic resistance to her mother's intrusiveness by refusing to take in her mother's literal food.

★　★　★

Annemarie came to therapy asking for my help in stopping her bingeing and achieving her goal of shedding one-hundred pounds. But it soon became apparent that Annemarie could barely take in anything I had to offer. She filled each of her sessions with elaborate descriptions of, and associations to, her dreams, forbidding me to comment, often speaking until the end of her session without pause. Over time, I came to understand that Annemarie's bingeing, and the added weight she carried as a result, symbolized her longing for, and memory of, her mother's *good milk*—the nurturance she had once received as an infant and small child—but had then been lost when she "stopped being cute." Annemarie longed to take in, to hold on to, to keep in the good food and good memories, splitting off the toxic and hurtful emotions that evolved with her mother's later rejection by telling herself "not to think about it." Unlike the perseverant yo-yo binge/dieter, who cyclically abandons hope that the containing other will return, the restrictor who stays chronically obese may be clinging to the memory of the early containment, holding onto the nurturance (in the form of the feeding) she once experienced, but trying to protect herself from further hurt by restricting painful feelings from entering or exiting her body/mind.

Amelia described her mother as "the baby whisperer," totally immersed in and dedicated to the care of her *newborns*, but increasingly uninterested as each of her six babies grew into toddlerhood and beyond. Amelia's home was filled with chaos, everyone but the newest infant left to fend for him or herself. Amelia began starving herself early in life—what we came to understand as her protest at the loss of her mother's care and attention, as well as her effort at restoring the sense of structure and regulation she had known as an infant.

Making use of protective psychic defense mechanisms not normally accessible until the more-developed second year of life—denial, dissociation, repression, and splitting—the 'restrictor' thus tries to help herself cope with the *loss* of attunement, whereas the perseverant spends her life *in search* of the attunement she has never been able to find. It is for this reason that I believe perseverant eating disorders pre-date and reflect an earlier emotional organization than restrictor disorders. Perseverant individuals have not developed the emotional tools or mechanisms to protect themselves from their fearfulness and dread. Uncontained from the beginning of life, they have remained—as W. R. Bion asserted—unable to "repress, suppress, or learn from experience" how to render their terror unconscious.[4] Like Kaitlin, they are left without the ability to avoid or distract their minds when they experience a disturbing or dysregulating state. They remain palpably aware of their longing and distress, their inability to protect themselves from its perseverative re-playing at the very core of their psychic disorganization.[5]

"An anorexic is afraid to take food in," I said to Kaitlin now, sensing her 'return' to the room. "And you are afraid to *keep* it in. In either case, the fear is that having food inside you, that 'containing' it in or on your body with no way to digest it, will make you horribly 'toxic'. What gets lost in the fear of *food* or the fear of *fat* is the *fear* itself. Fear has no calories and food has no magical power to make you bad."

"I just wish I could stick to my plan to not binge," Kaitlin said plaintively. "Why can't I make it through a day? It's like I don't know *how* to eat."

"Is it that you don't know *how* to eat, or that you don't know how to eat so it won't turn into a binge and purge?"

"That's it! It's like the minute I put anything in my mouth I tell myself it's all over: I don't have a choice. Once I've eaten, I *have* to purge, so I might as well binge."

"So that 'snap' in your brain doesn't just tell you to binge," I observed. "It also tells you that if you do, you can purge. You can stop feeling, stop trying to think. You can take a break, and deal with the problem later by purging the toxic feelings along with the food."

Kaitlin was pensive for several minutes, considering my words. "Last month," she said finally, "when Henry and I went on vacation for two weeks, I didn't throw up at all. I hardly even thought about throwing up. I wish I could get back to that feeling, to not be struggling all the time."

"What was it about those two weeks that made the difference?" I asked.

"Well, for one thing, I *knew* I couldn't throw up," Kaitlin responded. "Henry was with me every minute."

"So how did you eat during those two weeks?"

"*Very* carefully," she replied, "especially at the beginning. I thought about everything I put in my mouth."

"What were you thinking?"

"That I didn't want to gain weight; that I only had certain clothes with me and I wanted to make sure they fit. Henry did make a couple of comments about my not eating enough to keep a bird alive, but I explained to him that I was eating as much as I could comfortably handle without feeling like I needed to throw it up. He got it."

"So, it sounds like when you told yourself you *couldn't* throw up, you *thought* about everything you ate—what effect it would have on your body, and whether or not you were willing to put up with that effect."

"Yes, I guess that's right," Kaitlin considered this new perspective. "And truthfully, over the two weeks, I did start to feel a lot better. It got easier. I figured out how much I could eat and still be comfortable, and my clothes fit just fine—even though I was keeping in what felt like a lot of food. There were a couple of times when I felt like I had overdone it, but I was able to tell Henry about it, and he walked me through it."

"How did he do that?" I asked.

"I talked—no, I cried!—about how full I felt. One time, I ate too much *broccoli* and felt really full. I practically had a panic attack! Henry talked me off the ledge, reminding me that the feeling of fullness would pass and that nothing would happen to me; that I would be okay. We took a walk, and in a couple of hours I felt comfortable again. He was right. But since we've been home and he's been working so much, I'm struggling again."

"Being full of food is resolvable," I reflected. "Your body starts working on what you've eaten, breaking it down into usable nutriment. The feeling of fullness, as you discovered, passes in time. And allowing food to stay inside you also speeds up your metabolism, giving your body the work of digestion. Soon you discover that it doesn't take nearly as much as you thought to make you feel satisfied, and you can eat far more than you thought and remain comfortable with your body."

For Kaitlin, and others with perseverant binge/purge eating disorders, fullness was not a signal to stop eating or an indication of satiety. On the contrary, it meant that it was 'all over', that she had 'blown it', that she *had* to binge because she would *have* to purge anyway. Working to differentiate the physical and emotional experience of having food inside her, Kaitlin was trying to digest new variables: That when she had eaten enough to be satisfied, she would feel a sense of fullness in her stomach; that 'gut' feelings of pain, loneliness, and fear were different than hunger and the need for food. In her 'dysensithymic' experience, her inability to differentiate between felt-states or senses of her body and her mind both had felt the same. Until Kaitlin could differentiate the physical from the emotional, any sensation of 'fullness' would become a signal for evacuating 'toxicity'.

"What do you think would have happened if you felt you *could* throw up?" I asked her.

"Truthfully," Kaitlin said, "if I had known I could throw up, I would have missed the whole experience. All my thoughts on the trip would have been around what I could eat, how and where I could get rid of it, and how I could hide it from Henry. I probably would have withdrawn from him and missed the really great time we had together. We were so close. I felt so clear in my mind, not all foggy in the head like I usually feel when I've been purging. It really was a great feeling."

"So, what I'm hearing is that when you eat knowing you can purge, there is not only no *thinking* going on, but it actually contributes to your *difficulty* in thinking. The feelings that are feeding the binge get short-circuited; at best, they get put on hold. But when you decide that you *can't* purge, it actually frees-up your options. You slow down and make choices; you give yourself room to think about consequences. The feelings that aren't thrown up are right there for you to see. You can process them together, think them through yourself, write about or meditate on them. The feelings don't get cut off—and neither did Henry!"

The decision to stop purging, I have come to believe, is far more manageable for the patient seeking a resolution to cyclical bingeing and purging than are the repeated promises, attempts, and inevitable failures at giving up bingeing. Bingeing reflects the urgent—albeit no-longer-relevant—messages from the most primitive recesses of the mind—messages that insist that eating in the absence of nutritional need is necessary for thought-processing and critical to survival. Bingeing substitutes for thinking, and the illusion that it carries no consequences makes it a compelling option. In the face of dysregulating emotion of any stripe, the perseverant individual is hard pressed to avoid the 'tried-and-true' mode of processing emotion by way of the familiar cyclical process.

The informed and conscious decision to stop purging, on the other hand, opens the door to genuine thinking. It encourages considering what, when, and how one chooses to eat, whether eating is 'worth it', whether there are other options available. It encourages experimenting with new foods, new tastes, and learning how much can safely be eaten without triggering perseverative fear patterns in the brain. The decision not to purge paves the way for addressing emotions that have been left unfiltered and unprocessed over a lifetime—thoughts and feelings that have been blunted by the temporary anesthetic effect provided by food. Not purging means to *keep in*—not just food, but thoughts, relatedness, experiences. It means taking in the emotional nourishment provided by compliments, goodwill, expressions of love and care; it means developing the confidence that even unsavory input can be dealt with and survived. Waiting just those few extra seconds, allowing cortical thinking processes to kick in, alters the perseverative patterns. "Things," as Kaitlin put it, "just start to make more sense."

Bodies on their own, I often tell my patients, have no brains. Emotions can't be resolved by eating, and physical fullness is different than being full of undigested feelings. Similarly, undigested emotion can never be resolved by purging. For much as Kaitlin tried to get rid of toxic feelings by evacuating them physically, the attempt at finding a physical solution for her emotional problems ultimately didn't and couldn't work. It might take some Herculean leaps of faith until she became convinced that she wouldn't gain weight on broccoli or watermelon, or while feeding her body consciously when it was hungry. It might take an even greater leap of faith to recognize that the feelings in her body did not change or determine who she was as an individual. Her mind and body were intertwined, and our work on separating and differentiating them so they could work together was still a work-in-progress. But Kaitlin's efforts at holding on for those extra few moments until the urge to purge passed, holding on and allowing herself to feel the feelings beneath the surge, was a hopeful sign. She was beginning to think with her mind about her feelings, and her battle with food was moving toward a negotiated settlement.

## Notes

1   Bratman, S. & Knight, D. (2004). *Health Food Junkies: Orthorexia Nervosa—the Health Food Eating Disorder*. New York: Broadway Books.
2   Kullman, A. (2007). The 'perseverant' personality: A pre-attachment perspective on the etiology and evolution of binge/purge eating disorders. *Psychoanalytic Dialogues*, 17(5): 705–732.
3   Johnson, C. & Connors, M. (1987). *The Etiology and Treatment of Bulimia Nervosa: A Biopsychosocial Perspective*. New York: Basic Books.
4   Bion, W. R. (1962b). Learning from experience. In *Seven Servants: Four Works by Wilfred R. Bion*. Northvale, NJ: Jason Aronson, 1977, p. 8.
5   Kullman, A. (2007).

# *thinking interrupted*

JASMINE AVOIDED MY EYES as I greeted her in the waiting room. She walked past me without responding, entered the consulting room, and sat stiffly at the far end of the sofa. She was silent for several minutes.

"I'm *mad*," she finally said, her eyes dark and clouded. "I'm just *mad*. I've been coming here for . . . how many months now? And I'm still bingeing and purging. Maybe this just isn't working."

I sat quietly, nodding my encouragement, waiting to see where Jasmine's anger might take us. This wasn't the first time Jasmine had expressed frustration over the pace of her 'un-covery', but it felt by far the most intense. I understood how difficult it was for her to be patient: Un-covering an eating disorder from 'the inside out' is not short-term work, frequently involving starts and stops as the brain adapts to new pathways and possibilities. Learning to hold onto her mind rather than trying to 'think' with her body when she was anxious or upset took time—and extraordinary perseverance.

"Are you just going to sit there?" Jasmine demanded.

"I can imagine how frustrating this must be for you, Jasmine," I ventured, "and how mad you are about still having to struggle sometimes. What do you think that might be about right now?"

"What do I think *what* is about," she retorted coldly, and I instantly felt like I was in the presence of the biting sarcasm she had described as her mother's "signature." This must be what it had been like for her all these years, I thought to myself. I suspected that she needed me to know exactly what she had experienced. It was not pleasant.

Jasmine stared at me accusingly, waiting for my reply.

"What do *you* think is going on?" I asked, trying to keep my voice even. "Why do *you* think you are still bingeing and purging?"

"I don't *know* why!" she snapped. "Isn't that *your* job, to figure out *why*?"

I was aware of the growing tension in my body. The analyst part of me recognized the importance of this moment: Jasmine's usually well-concealed anger making its appearance in the consulting room. I knew that moving beyond her eating disorder would require her to un-cover the rage and rebellion she had been denied as a child and adolescent. She needed to dis-cover whether her anger would destroy me or our relationship, whether I would retaliate or be resentful of her, or send her packing like her mother unfortunately had. Nevertheless, I admitted wistfully to myself, it sure felt better when Jasmine thought I was wonderful!

I have learned to expect and *respect* occasional or even sustained bouts of anger from my eating disorder patients. Disconcerting as it may seem in the moment, these expressions of raw emotion—of frustration or anger or blame—are essential ingredients of the 'un-covery' process. For some, therapy stirs up wounds so deeply-embedded, or experienced as so intolerable, that they must be 'purged' or projected outward, sometimes onto any available 'object'—literal or figurative. For some, casting off the familiar role of 'perfect' or 'compliant' child (or patient) is essential, unmasking deeper feelings in search of their still-unidentified destinations. And sometimes a breach may be the result of our own *real* relationship: Something I have said or done may unexpectedly affect my patient and cause a rupture. Such an occurrence, in fact, is such a predictable event in the 'un-covery' process that often at the beginning of our work together I give my patients a 'head's up': "There will come a time," I tell them "not *if*, but *when*, that I may unintentionally say or do something that angers or upsets you. *Those* are the times when it is especially important for you not to go underground, to let me know *exactly* what happened, and how you feel about it. We may learn more from the times I inadvertently misunderstand or upset you than we may from all the times I get it just right."

For the perseverant individual who has not learned from experience about the nuances and rhythms of relationships, any breach in attuned connec-tion may seem or become catastrophic—even potentially destroying the therapeutic alliance. Jasmine's expression of deeply-felt thoughts or feelings, in whatever form it was taking, was thus an important developmental achievement for her, an integral part of her 'un-covery'.

"You sound pretty angry at me, Jasmine," I said finally. "Like you think I'm falling down on the job."

"Yes, I'm angry!" she replied sarcastically, still staring at me relentlessly. "*I've* been doing *my* part."

"Then you must believe that I haven't been doing mine."

Jasmine moved closer to the edge of the sofa, suddenly looking as if she was not quite sure whether to bolt or burst into tears. "Maybe this just isn't working," her voice trembled. "Maybe I just need to go to cognitive therapy and get a ten-point program after all."

"You think there's someone out there who would be better than I am at helping you," I offered, inviting the transference into our conversation. Jasmine had spent her entire life longing for a mother who would finally "get" her. Any failure to intuit her needs would inevitably re-open those wounds. Helping her recognize how these unresolved longings were still impacting her relationships was critical to our work together.

"Perhaps you are disappointed in me," I added quietly.

"So, are you saying it's my fault?" she demanded.

"I don't recall saying it was anybody's fault," I risked a small smile. "It is what it is. These are the feelings you are having, and it would be good if we could work them through together. Are you afraid that you and I can't work this out?" I gambled.

"I don't know *what* I think anymore!" Jasmine's clenched fists pounded the sofa. Tears erupted out of the sides of her dark eyes.

"I have tried and I have tried!" she sputtered. "I have tried eating 'safe' foods and I have tried only eating when I'm hungry. I have tried every which way to Tuesday! But I still end up like last night, bingeing and purging."

"You have tried, and on many days, you have succeeded," I pointed out. "Can you tell me what happened last night?"

"I don't *want* to talk about last night!" she insisted. "I'm sick of trying to figure this out! I just want it to stop!" Jasmine flung her body into the back of the sofa and closed her eyes. We sat together in silence for several long minutes.

"My father wants me to quit," she said finally, not looking at me.

"Ohhh," I said, exhaling deeply, simultaneously relieved to know what we were dealing with, but concerned about a potential breach in Jasmine's support system. "Did that come up before or after you binged and purged?"

"Both," she said. "He's been hinting at it for weeks. But we had a big fight about it last night."

"Ahh" I said softly, resonating now with the defeat I heard in her voice. Her father had been hinting about it for weeks, I noted to myself, and Jasmine had been carrying it around alone. She hadn't been able to tell me about it: A prescription for emotional disaster. What had kept her from sharing it?

Small wonder she was struggling. She no doubt had fallen back into looking to food when conflict had overwhelmed her mind and made it impossible for her to think.

"What was the fight about?"

"I was defending you," she said. "I told my father I was going to do whatever I wanted, and if he wouldn't help me, I would ask my grandmother or go get a job."

"Why did you need to defend me?" I asked. "It must have made you really angry to feel like you had to defend me."

Jasmine looked at me, as if surprised by my response. "He was saying that I should be completely over this by now. He said that I've been coming long enough, and if this was going to work, it would have by now."

"I wonder whether part of you also began to wonder whether your father wasn't right."

Jasmine again looked surprised. "It's hard to justify this expense when I'm not getting any better," she said, her icy demeanor now on thaw.

"*Are* you *not* getting any better?"

"Well, I thought I was. At least I can go to school now and not stay home all day and binge and purge. I hadn't binged or purged for almost six weeks before last night. Just because he saw me eat a little more for dinner last night, he went bonkers. I tried to tell him that I was experimenting with how much I could eat and still stay comfortable. I *told* him that I wasn't going to purge, but he wouldn't believe me. I'm just so sick of arguing with him about this. Maybe it's just better if I quit and work on it by myself."

Jasmine, I could hear, had collided with an unanticipated obstacle at a critical juncture in her 'un-covery': The possible loss of the emotional support she needed in her everyday life to help bolster the efforts she was making in her therapy. Much as family and friends may be eager for their loved one to recover, they are often unprepared for the changes and challenges that are inevitable aspects of 'un-covering' an eating disorder. Over the years I have encountered many such conundrums: Parents of anorexics who complain about the food budget, just as their child begins to eat normal portions; spouses or parents who insist on their loved one cutting back on sessions, just as critical issues begin to emerge; patients themselves who become frightened by their own empowerment or fearful of life without their familiar mode of processing emotion. Jasmine no longer sat quietly or acquiesced to the ideas of others or to circumstances she felt were unfair. In addition to experimenting with how much she could comfortably eat, she also was listening to and making connection with her own thoughts and feelings, expressing them, standing up for herself, taking part in conversations she would previously have avoided—like the one we were having now. Jasmine was taking risks with relationships—something that for me pointed to her growing sense of safety in the world—challenging the need for the solitary thinking and eating represented by her eating disorder.

"Sometimes it doesn't feel like I'm getting any better," she said, her eyes again filling with tears. "I get so frustrated, I don't know what else to do. Maybe I just can't do it. Maybe I just have to be this way for the rest of my life."

"I understand how it could feel that way, Jasmine," I said, sensing the return of our deep connection. Indeed, I understood her ambivalence—a natural and predictable side-effect of therapy: Wanting it and not wanting it; longing for connection, and being wary of it; the seeming unreasonableness of having to 'pay' for a relationship; the slow pace of unearthing deeply-rooted emotional wounds and memories. Maintaining a relationship with others, staying mindful, even sustaining a connection with one's own thinking mind, can at times be brutal for the individual working at un-covering an eating disorder—and the purveyor of such notions (i.e., the therapist) can easily be perceived as an impediment to relief. Jasmine was not only primed to take care of her needs on her own, but to do so instantaneously. Learning to delay gratification, to be patient, to trust that a difficult moment would pass, to learn new ways of coping with extreme pressure or distress, were all elements of a work-in-progress. Sometimes months of effort could seem to disappear in a heartbeat, and identifying the issues that caused a breach or a re-lapse in thinking could be challenging. Jasmine, like most of my perseverant patients, had little experience in navigating the rhythms of relatedness, the sequence of mis-connection, dis-connection, and repair. She was learning the language of connection from scratch, and was inevitably hitting those seemingly unresolvable forks in the road.

"Perhaps there are options other than blaming yourself or blaming me," I suggested to her now. "Maybe if we talked about what's been happening, we could find other possibilities."

"But that's all we *do* is talk!"

"Yes, I guess that's mostly true," I agreed. "But it sounds like we only talk about *some* things."

"What do you mean?" she asked, looking at me warily.

"Well, for example, you mentioned earlier that your father has been on you for weeks to quit, but you haven't talked about that in here with me.

That must have been a really hard thing for you to carry alone. You were left to think on your own, and I wonder whether it might have thrown you back on your old reliance on food to help you think."

"Oh!" Jasmine gasped. "I didn't think about that."

Jasmine had gotten lost trying to understand the nature of her distress. She couldn't figure out how and why a breach had occurred between us —or even whether that breach was indeed about us. She didn't know whether she 'should' or 'shouldn't' feel as she did. Her perseverant thinking had conspired to keep her locked in her solitary 'autizoid' world. It had not occurred to her that we could think together and arrive at a shared understanding—even about such highly-charged subjects as our own relationship.

Thinking interrupted—or 'indigestion', as I sometimes call it—is not uncommon in the treatment of eating disorders, and for both patient and therapist, finding a balance can sometimes turn stomachs into knots. An eating disorder is a compelling force, and parting ways with it can be a tremendous challenge —both physically and emotionally. Some patients come to therapy believing they are ready to 'get over' their eating disorders, but have not banked on 'getting through' them—that is, weathering the "emotional storms" that are often needed to take them to the other side. The eating disorder has taken the edge off living; its instant gratification has made the intolerable seem tolerable, at least for a time. Coming to understand and combat the lure of that eating disorder can be more than they bargained for.

Some individuals may become disappointed when an apparent 'flight into health' or sudden 'spontaneous' recovery early in treatment proves to be short-lived, leaving them to mistakenly conclude that 'talk therapy' or in-depth exploration of the underlying dynamics won't be much more helpful than the brief psychotherapy or self-help strategies they have previously tried. Others may grow frustrated with the slower pace of dynamic psychotherapy and pre-emptively withdraw from treatment. While for some patients cost can be dealt with as a practical matter at the beginning of therapy, and/or re-visited as necessary, for others a sudden financial crisis may signal conscious or unconscious conflicts, roadblocks to 'un-covery' they may or may not be able or willing to work through. For some, being in an emotionally-attached relationship with a therapist may evoke grief or overwhelming conflict over their own absent significant (m)others; for others, the stress of ongoing relatedness may feel intolerable. The proverbial possibilities are endless. Staying open to the immediate circumstances surrounding whatever conflicts they may encounter—inside or outside of the consulting room—invariably offers the best opportunity to repair and sustain the therapeutic alliance.

For those individuals like Jasmine, whose 'indigestion' takes the form of a sudden re-emergence of the eating disorder symptom after a sustained period of 'un-covery', gentle exploration of the precipitating factors may prevent a total reversal of course. Inevitably, 'something' has happened, and the ability—not always possible—to ferret out the details offers the best hope for helping these individuals stay on track. Some patients think they should cut back, when actually they need *more frequent* contact to help bolster their efforts. Some worry when long-hidden 'negative' emotions erupt and disrupt their perceptions of themselves—or fear that the expression of true feelings might alienate needed others. Encouraging these individuals to express themselves openly, to not be concerned with 'hurting feelings' is particularly important with perseverant individuals, who are so accustomed to holding and storing their own toxic feelings, turning them against themselves, and then 'evacuating' them by way of their eating disorder. I often tell patients that the most important time to attend sessions is when they would rather not come, and the most important things to tell me are the things they would rather not say. It is only by way of small openings into hearts and minds that conflicted internal worlds begin to make sense, that thinking and eating can be differentiated from one another, and that the psychic blueprint that fosters an eating disorder can be redrawn.

"You spent six weeks thinking with your mind," I reminded Jasmine now. "In that time, you discovered and un-covered many things about yourself. What happened with your Dad last night sent you over the edge; it let you know the limits of your current capacity for thinking on your own, especially when you were facing the loss of a primary source of support. All the more reason to explore it, to understand what that limit was, and what you can do in the future."

Jasmine listened silently.

"You were hoping the food would help you think," I suggested after several minutes, considering how food had stepped in to rescue her, to replace the disorienting thoughts the fight with her father had stirred up. "Did it work?"

Jasmine shook her head. "No," she said. "I felt awful. Just like I always used to feel. I only slept for about an hour and woke up feeling puffy and drugged."

"Perhaps it would be helpful if we talked about what you would like your Dad to know about your therapy," I suggested. "What it means to you. And then maybe we could talk about what exactly happened last night and how it ended up making you feel so bad."

Jasmine looked at me intently, and I had the distinct impression that she was surprised I was still there. I knew that she was at a crossroads. She needed to make a decision—whether to push on into the unknown and frightening 'two-person' territory of relatedness—where outcomes are unpredictable, people disappoint, and anxiety needs to be tolerated—or stay locked in her own solitary, perseverant world, caught in the 'closed-circuit loop' of her eating disorder. Over many years of practice, I have seen people go both ways. Some, unable or unready to take the risk, leave therapy. Some leave and return, renewing contact weeks, months, or even years later when they are ready to pick up where they left off. Still others traverse the 'rocky road' and come out on the other side. I didn't yet know which path Jasmine would choose.

As our session came to an end, Jasmine's eyes once again filled with tears. I walked with her silently to the door.

"I'll see you Thursday?" she asked.

"Absolutely," I replied.

For the moment, it seemed, we had dodged a bullet.

# *thinking and linking*

SOMETIMES AN UNEXPECTED moment of clarity can be transformational:

"I have to tell you what happened to me on Sunday!" Susie was excited once again, eager to begin her session. It had been more than two years since we had begun our work together, and I had come to anticipate and appreciate her sudden bursts of enthusiasm as heralding significant shifts in her thinking and her life. In the time we had spent working together, Susie had completed her school program and earned a degree. She had been holding down a job, and despite her mother's warnings not to marry for fear of "passing on her genes," was in a 'real' relationship for the first time in her life. While Susie's circular thinking was still apparent—particularly when her emotions stretched her capacity to contain them—her ability to think together, to take in, keep in, and maintain links with others were all steadily growing.

"So, I went to Maine to visit my relatives over the weekend," Susie proceeded. "On the way back, I had to change planes in New York. I *hate* flying out of New York. I've gotten stuck there so many times. One time we sat on the tarmac for *four hours*, with no air conditioning, no food or drinks, and they wouldn't even let us off the plane! It was awful."

I nodded sympathetically, appreciating Susie's colorful way of describing her life.

"So before we left Maine, I wanted to make sure I had enough food with me. I brought an apple with me from my aunt's house, and then in the airport I bought a banana and some coffee. Then I thought, just in case, I should get a muffin and some trail mix, just to have with me. The flight was delayed, so I ate the apple and banana while I was waiting, and then just before boarding, I bought another banana to replace the first one, and then I ate the muffin. Normally, I don't eat anywhere near that much food, especially early in the morning, but I felt this anxiety in me. When we finally got to New York, there was a layover of about an hour-and-a-half. I wasn't hungry, but I decided to buy a salad, just in case I got hungry on the cross-country flight. The salads were small, so I bought two of them, just to have with me."

"*Just in case.*" "*Just to have with me.*" I was beginning to hear a pattern.

"Miraculously," Susie rolled her eyes, "the plane left the gate on time. But then—would you believe it!—we got stuck on the tarmac because of thunder and lightning! We waited in the plane for *two hours* before they finally let us return to the gate. While we were still in the plane, I opened the trail mix—which I would *never* have ordinarily eaten—and I ate it all. *Then*, when we got back to the terminal to wait out the storm, I bought another salad, even though I hadn't eaten the first two, and a bagel and another muffin. By then I had two huge sacks of food that I was carrying around, enough to feed the entire Greek Army!"

Susie looked over at me, checking for my reaction. I nodded, encouraging her to go on.

"It was at that point that I realized that this was very crazy," Susie grew intently serious. "That it really wasn't normal at all. I walked around for a while and I kept checking in with myself about whether I was hungry, and I could feel that I wasn't at all. And that's when I knew—*really* knew—that this didn't have anything to do with food. It was something much bigger."

"What were you thinking?"

"I remember being afraid that they would call for re-boarding and I wouldn't have enough time to get more food. I remember debating between buying food that I usually eat—like salads or fruit—or buying heavier foods that would keep me full—like another bagel or muffin—that I could eat just in case something happened. And then," she added, as if remembering a new piece of the puzzle, "I also remember being worried that some of the fresher foods, like the salad or fresh fruit, might make me sick on the plane. There have been so many salmonella scares lately. I started to feel this frenzy, like I didn't know what to do."

"It sounds like you were afraid that you were in extreme danger," I reflected. "You were worried about your safety and how and whether you could take care of yourself."

"Yes. I remember the feeling, the fear. It wasn't exactly panic, but close to it. If I hadn't been able to get enough food, I would have been scared to death. I'm always afraid of what will happen to me." Susie paused. "But I also remember feeling that there was something really wrong with the way I was thinking; that food wasn't what I really needed."

"What do you think you really needed?"

"Something to reassure me," she said. "Something to make me feel like I was going to be okay."

I noted the "*something*"—rather than the *someone*—that was still Susie's automatic, unconscious response.

"You were afraid of not having the supplies you needed to survive." I proposed. "Afraid you would be left on the 'emotional tarmac', so to speak, without anyone or anything to protect you."

"Food has always been my protector," she replied. "At least that's what I've thought all these years. But this time, I could really see that I was scared. I was afraid of being alone on the plane and having something happen."

"Being helpless . . . and alone."

"Yes, that's exactly it. Being helpless and alone."

I waited silently, wondering what other associations might occur to Susie.

"I work so hard trying to look like I'm like everyone else," she said slowly. "It's like I don't want anyone to know how scared I am. I hate flying alone, even though I do it all the time. It's like I have no control over what might happen to me."

Susie had indeed spent her life "flying alone," I thought to myself, trying her best to think her way through the terror and helplessness that were as embedded in her body/mind as they were mirrored in her eating disorder. The cumulative traumatic experiences had lived on in her implicit, non-verbal memory, re-awakened particularly by situations over which she had little control. The fear/terror alarm bells that went off in her mind were powerful stimulants. Without realizing it, Susie had stockpiled food in her desperate attempt at quelling the catastrophic fear that overwhelmed her far more frequently than she had ever imagined.

"How did you think the food would protect you?" I asked her.

"That's the thing," she replied. "I think it was the first time I could really see that it couldn't have. When I looked down and realized I was carrying around two huge sacks of food, like an arsenal, I knew that it was a fantasy that I've lived with my whole life. I was afraid of being afraid. And I was acting as if the food could help, as if it could save me. For the first time, I could see that there could never be *enough* food on the face of the planet to keep me feeling safe. There could never be enough."

★   ★   ★

"Enough" was a theme that also ran through every arena of Lucie's life. Though Lucie had stopped bingeing and purging months before, un-covering the fears that fostered her bulimia continued to keep us engaged. Lucie feared she would run out of food if she didn't pack *enough* before she left for work. She worried that her apartment wouldn't be clean *enough* when her parents came to visit. She feared she wouldn't have *enough* clothing with her on a trip, that she wouldn't be thin *enough* at her high school reunion, that she wouldn't be prepared *enough* when she made a presentation.

"I'm always afraid I won't have or be enough," Lucie fretted, conscious of her own disturbing pattern.

"I hear you focusing on the word 'enough'," I reflected. "But for me, the operative word is 'afraid'. You are *afraid* that you won't be okay, that you won't survive, that you won't feel like you have or *are* enough to preserve yourself."

Lucie had never been enough for her mother. She had grown up in fear that there wouldn't be enough to feed her, physically or emotionally. A new-born baby learns from her experiences that there will be enough when she has repeated experiences of there actually *being* enough. She gets hungry, she cries, she gets fed, and she feels better. If she receives a 'full' meal—the food along with the soothing and nurturing she needs—she feels satisfied and has enough. She learns from her experiences that bad feelings don't last forever, that they can be soothed and sated. But if she receives but 'half-a-meal'—or a resentment-filled one—nothing ever feels quite enough.

Together Lucie and I unpacked her fears:

"What would happen if you didn't have enough clothing with you on your trip?" I asked.

"I guess I could buy some while I was there," she replied. "When you put it that way, it sounds so simple. I mean, I won't die or anything. They sell clothing where I'm going! Or I could even do a laundry if I needed to."

"And what will happen if you aren't thin enough at your reunion?"

"People will think things about me," she tensed up. "My old classmates will think, 'Oh there's Lucie. She's really packed on the pounds'."

"And then what will happen?"

Lucie looked at me, bewildered. "I'll be laughed at," she said. "Just like I was as a child. People will talk behind my back about how fat I am. I will feel humiliated."

"And what if you feel humiliated?"

Lucie was stumped. "I don't know."

"You will feel bad, I imagine. It will sting. But then what will happen?"

"I guess I will survive," she looked surprised. "I guess my life will move on and something else will happen. It always does."

"Exactly!" I applauded her realization.

Lucie thought for a moment. "It sort of reminds me of the way I stopped bingeing and purging," she said. "I asked myself, 'What will happen if you get hungry? And I told myself, 'If you're hungry, you can eat till you've had enough, and then if you get hungry again, you can eat again. And if you're full, you can stop and not eat until you feel hungry. It's okay. You'll be okay'."

"Yes!" I exclaimed. "That's it!"

Lucie was learning more each day about the powerful grip food had had on her psyche, and how greatly she had been dependent on food and 'the feeding' to provide her with "enough" resources to manage her unmanageable and un-imaginable fears. Lucie had taken another major step toward 'un-covering' the roots and dis-covering the fears that had fueled her eating disorder. Thinking together, her mind was untangling from her body, and food was separating from thought.

★   ★   ★

Almost a year after she stopped bingeing and purging, Charlotte decided to attend a ten-day silent meditation retreat. Working on meditation together in sessions had given Charlotte a new-found sense of calmness and confidence in her ability to manage her emotions and her eating, and she was eager to go even deeper into connecting her body and her mind. But during the retreat, Charlotte had an unanticipated traumatic experience. Though everyone had taken a vow of silence, Charlotte had the distinct impression that some of the women didn't like her. Every time she sat down at the community dining table, two or three of the women would pick up their trays and move elsewhere. The sense of rejection and humiliation filled Charlotte with almost unbearable pain and shame, triggering her lifelong despair at being unknown, unwanted, and misunderstood.

"The first two days," Charlotte told me, "I cried when I was meditating and when I was walking and when I was eating. I felt as alone as I've ever felt in my life. By the end of the third day, I came to the realization that there were three words that had cast a shadow over my entire life: '*Nobody likes me*'. It just made me cry and cry all the more. I could feel the grief of my whole life."

Charlotte reached for a tissue. "But then," she said, a new determination in her voice, "I started to think about how I had *always* felt as alone as I was feeling right then. I had just covered it up by eating, or trying to act in ways that I hoped would make people like me better. Then, when something happened and I felt like an outsider again, I'd feel like not only was my *real* self not any good, but even my *fake* self couldn't make people like me. It's strange, though," her voice quivered with emotion. "At the retreat, I couldn't talk to anyone. I felt filled with sadness and grief, but I had to hold it all myself, inside me. There was nothing I could do but sit and be with it. I couldn't eat to take the edge off it; I just needed to be *in* myself. I sort of talked to you in my mind—I could feel you there with me—but other than that, I felt totally alone. Then, it's like the heavens suddenly opened. It suddenly occurred to me that even if no one liked me, I still had myself. There I was, surviving, with just myself to rely on. Yes, I was alone, but for the first time in my life I didn't *feel* alone or afraid. I didn't feel any need for food, or the need to find a way to make the pain and sadness go away. I started to feel stronger. By the last day, I reached the conclusion that I couldn't control how anyone else felt about me. They either liked me or they didn't, or maybe they liked some things about me and not others. Either way, I still had myself. I could still survive, just like I had that week. I was going to be okay."

Charlotte had spent her life in terror that she really would be alone—not just *fear* being alone—and not be able to survive it. What she discovered during her retreat was that she had the capacity to tolerate being with herself; that she could think with her thoughts, feel with her feelings, nourish her body, and survive them all. The payoff for experiencing the reality of her pain was a newly-emerging sense of calm that was replacing the desperation she had lived with for as long as she could remember. Charlotte had walked through life with her version of 'the truth', her 'theory of mind', worrying what others might think of her, fearful that those negative perceptions were true. Allowing herself to *lean into* her truth, into her fear; to think with her thoughts, rather than stifle and mask them by eating, was opening new vistas for her. Charlotte wasn't 're-covering' her fears by finding ways of distracting herself; she was *un-covering* the roots that had fueled her eating disorder and left her living a fearful and shame-filled life.

★ ★ ★

Susie, Lucie, and Charlotte were each well on their way to picking up the developmental pieces of their childhoods where they had been lost, identifying, making, and maintaining the kinds of emotional connections to themselves and others they had longed for, and developing the tools and strategies they needed to enhance their tolerance for living within their own bodies and minds. Each, in her own way, was traversing the path of 'uncovery', transforming the fear-filled perseveration of her eating disorder into the capacity to think with her thoughts, make links with others, and discover ways of living a far more nourishing and fulfilling life.

Ultimately, learning to think with the mind rather than the body is an ongoing process. Thinking provides a new sense of stability and groundedness that changes the architecture of a perseverant individual's mind, even as it challenges *perseveration* with the *perseverance* needed for living a more meaningful and connected life. Letting go of the *symptom* of bingeing and purging often means that all the reasons it was needed to begin with make themselves known. Each individual has to grapple with the reality that she may have little control over things outside of herself, that she can't expect the world to always go as she plans, that she can't anticipate everything that might impact her. All she is able to control are her own actions and reactions. Working together to develop the tools for thinking, the capacity for feeling, and the words to express them all helps establish a new base of operations, a central core that makes it safe to stay conscious, to explore even the most challenging aspects of living without losing oneself.

As one former patient told me nearly twenty years after the conclusion of our work together, life after an eating disorder is neither magical nor without its complications. Nevertheless, she said, "Bulimia never even occurs to me. I have watched so many people struggle with eating disorders over the years, 'white-knuckling' it, as you used to call it. I've never struggled. You taught me that an eating disorder is a metaphor and I never forgot it. I once asked you how long it would take me to get over it, and you said, 'You don't get over an eating disorder; you go *through* it'. And that was just the way it was."

# epilogue

MEGAN WAS LATE. Fifteen minutes late, in fact. Waiting for her in my office, I was aware of how unusual this was for her, how religiously she had always kept her appointments, almost always arriving precisely at her scheduled time. Re-checking my phone, I found no new messages. I picked up a book, but found myself distracted by a vague sense of unease.

The light indicating her arrival finally lit up at twenty past the hour. I opened the door to find Megan looking disheveled, her tailored black suit rumpled, scuffed black pumps in her hands. Absent were any of her usual accoutrements—the large leather handbag, the briefcase, the armload of papers she frequently carried with her. I held open the door and she walked silently past me and into the inner office.

"Well," she said, looking exhausted as she dropped onto the sofa, "It's done. It's over. I left, walked out. I'm never going back."

"You've left?" The question hung in the tension-filled air. Left her husband? Her job? Her family?

"I walked out of a deposition," she said, her voice trembling, but determined. "I just couldn't take it anymore." She reached for a tissue. "All of a sudden, I realized why the managing partner and my father were so intent on having me in on this case. I felt like such a *fool*."

Megan shifted positions on the couch, as if she could not bear to be in her own skin. When she pushed her hair away from her face, I noticed the tears pooling in her dark eyes.

"This man," she said, her voice breaking. "This sad, tired, gray-looking man just crumpled, right before my eyes. His wife was having trouble breathing and he was rushing her to the hospital. He hit the brakes hard when he realized he couldn't make it through a yellow light and the passenger-seat airbag went off and hit his wife right in the face and chest. And she died! Right there in the car, right in front of him, and he couldn't do a thing to help her!"

Megan burst into tears. I sat in silence, riveted by her words, by the intensity of her emotion.

Megan swallowed hard and quickly wiped away her tears. "And do you know what I was supposed to do?" she asked, the anger once again rising in her voice. "I was supposed to go in and 'soften him up', get him to relax, let him think he could trust me 'like his daughter', they said. Then, when the *real lawyers* came in, they would nail him. Wasn't it *his* fault for slamming on the brakes? '*Our client has an unsurpassed safety record*'," she mimicked her co-counsel. "'*Isn't it true that you were driving erratically? You were speeding, weren't you! What kind of a man would speed with a sick wife in the car? And, when did you last have your car serviced? You were overdue, sir, weren't you!*' The man kept trying to explain, to defend himself, like he really was worried that it was his fault. And his attorney just sat there and let them take him apart!"

Megan rose from the couch and walked across the room. She poured a glass of water from the pitcher on the side table.

"So, I walked out," she said, her voice now gaining in steadiness and determination. "I got up and walked straight out the door and out of the office and down the elevator and out to the street and I started running, in my high heels, all the way to the bay. And I just sat there, I don't know for how long. Suddenly, I looked at my watch and realized I was late and I didn't have a thing with me—not my purse or my phone or money or *anything*. So, I walked here." She paused. "Would you mind if I used your phone to call Jon and let him know I'm alright?"

"Of course," I replied, handing her my phone.

Megan spoke softly into the phone, apologizing to Jon for not calling him, reassuring him that she was okay, arranging for him to pick her up at my office. Realizing that it must have been several hours since she had left her office without money or resources, I asked Megan if she was hungry. She gratefully accepted a protein bar and some tea, and curled her legs beneath her on the couch.

"What were you thinking about when you were at the bay," I asked her.

"I was thinking about my whole life," she replied. "How I've spent my whole life trying to fit into my parents' world. I did everything I could to please them, to be the girl other people thought I ought to be. But today, it suddenly didn't matter anymore. I looked at that man and saw how he was being manipulated, how he was being made to feel like it was all *his* fault, and suddenly I saw *myself.* This is *my* life, I thought. Not only what was done to me, but what I was now being a part of doing to someone else!"

Megan leaned forward and set her tea on the table. "Everything inside me just shut down in that room," she said. "I just knew I couldn't do it anymore. I couldn't keep being the 'good girl' and pass the manipulation on. I couldn't keep turning a blind eye to what it does to other people . . . or to me."

I was deeply moved by Megan's words and actions, knowing how much courage it had taken for her to stand up to what had been the blueprint for her life. Megan was saying 'no' to far more than the charade in the law office conference room. She was saying 'no' to a lifetime of taking in toxic elements, 'no' to the manipulations that had colored her world miserable, 'no' to living a lie. This seemingly 'sudden' moment of enlightenment had taken her months and months of painstaking work to achieve.

"I know that, in his own way, my father loves me," she said, after several moments of silence. "I know in his mind, all of this is for me. He would tell you that everything he does is so his children will be 'set' for the rest of their lives. I've tried to make his dreams come true. But I just can't live my life his way anymore. I have this feeling of *truth* inside me, this sense that what is happening is *real*. It's this feeling of certainty—not even anger—just *certainty* that I am not going to play the game anymore.

Megan sat silently again for several minutes. "You know," she said quietly, "I came here saying that I can't go on living this way, but now, for the first time, I really know why. I'm not willing to hide anymore. I won't keep acting as if I'm 'all together'. I'm sick of all this. Bulimia has been my crutch and I guess I've needed it. It has been the only way I could keep doing what I was doing. But now . . . I don't need crutches anymore. Now I can walk. Now it's just in my way. It just feels over."

There was a quality to Megan's voice unlike any I had heard in her before. Megan had had her share of "false stops," as she called them. There were days and weeks when she had been able to stop bingeing and purging. But "something" had always happened that had sent her back into the cyclical patterns, leaving her filled with the familiar despair and remorse. This day seemed different.

"I know I've said this before," she said, looking at me, "but I really don't want to live in hiding anymore. I don't want to be numb. I don't want to lie or avoid the truth. I don't want to be the fraud I've always been afraid people will think I am."

Megan took in a deep breath.

"I'm going to stop," she exhaled.
And she did.

Several months later, as Megan and I slowly walked to the door on the last day of her therapy, I thought about how she had lived a lifetime trying to calm her fears, to soothe her injuries, with a balm that had only deepened her wounds. She had lived in fear of feeling her fear—the fear of being alone, of being abandoned, helpless, unconnected. Food had grounded her; it had been her most trusted companion. It had served as the living conduit for her longing, her hunger, and the myriad emotions for which she had had no words. Eating without thinking had nurtured her terror. Now thinking without eating had given her substance and sustenance. It had given her a renewed life, fresh air to breathe. Megan's hunger for connection, at long last, was finally being fed.

# glossary

**autizoid** a solitary, 'one-person psychology', set in motion when an infant is unable to achieve a needed psychic connection to a "living" "object-other" (mother) beginning with the earliest feedings of life. Results in attachment to an "inanimate object," (food and the feeding) as the primary source of containment and nurturance, and "thinking alone" as the primary mode of thought processing and emotional regulation (See Kullman, 1995).

**dysensithymia (dys-sensi-thymia)** an impairment in the ability to distinguish between felt-states or senses of body and mind. Accounts for such phenomena as the replacement of normally intact thinking with 'food thoughts' in the face of overwhelming emotional experiences, the conflation of internal or 'gut' feelings with sensations of hunger, and the *literal* use of food for thought.

**dyslexithymia (dys-lexi-thymia)** an impairment in the ability to make use of language and its nuances to capture the essence of, extract meaning from, and/or make emotional connection with the words assigned to one's experiences.

**emotional/relational dyslexia** a perseverative *over-investment* in the nature, nuance, and meaning of interpersonal modes of communication and relatedness (see also 'relational rumination').

**one-person psychology** a solitary mode of thinking and relating that develops in the absence of a containing other (See also 'autizoid'; see Kullman, 1995, 2007).

**mutual re-cog-nition** (as I use it) a conjoint exchange of emotion and cognition shared by the mother/infant dyad (See Kullman, 1995).

**perseverant personality** a solitary and circular mode of being, thinking, and relating that is organized around a sustained physical and emotional reliance on the feeding as a means of thought processing and emotional regulation (See Kullman, 2007).

**relational rumination**   a function of 'emotional/relational dyslexia' (see above), includes an intense desire to *know*, to read between the lines of meaning, to decode or deconstruct the emotional undercurrents of every interaction and communication.

**restrictor disorders**   eating disorders that are organized around the need to restrict or *keep out* either emotion and/or the food that symbolizes it.

**toxic container**   the cornerstone of body dysmorphia, low self-esteem, and self-hatred characteristic of binge/purge and other eating disorders, whereby 'uncontained' toxic distress is held and stored inside the body/mind, the individual comes to identify with it, and subsequently sees him/herself as bad or toxic (See Kullman, 1995; 2007).

**un-covery**   the achievement of a life-changing understanding of the underlying dynamics of a perseverant pattern and the development of new ways of thought processing and emotional regulation that allows for the replacement of 'perseveration' with the 'perseverance' to live a more nourishing life; the antidote to the solitary and circular mode of thought processing that characterizes a lifetime of 'thinking' with the body.

# bibliography

Ainsworth, M. & Bell, S. (1969). Some contemporary patterns of mother–infant interaction in the feeding situation. In A. Ambrose (ed.), *Stimulation in early infancy*. New York: Academic Press, 1969, pp. 133–170.

Aron, L. (2000). Self-reflexivity and the therapeutic action of psychoanalysis. *Psychoanalytic Psychology*, 17(4): 667–689.

Beebe, B. & Lachmann, F. (1994). Representations and internalization in infancy: Three principles of salience. *Psychoanalytic Psychology*, 11: 127–165.

Berra, Y. (1998). *The Yogi Book: I Really Didn't Say Everything I Said!* New York: Workman Publishing.

Bion, W. R. (1959). Attacks on linking. In *Second Thoughts: Selected Papers on Psychoanalysis*. Northvale, NJ: Jason Aronson, 1967, pp. 93–109.

—— (1962a). A theory of thinking. In *Second Thoughts: Selected Papers on Psychoanalysis*. Northvale, NJ: Jason Aronson, 1967, pp. 110–119.

—— (1962b). Learning from experience. In *Seven Servants: Four Works by Wilfred R. Bion*. Northvale, NJ: Jason Aronson, 1977, pp. 1–111.

Bowlby, J. (1969). *Attachment and Loss, Vol. I: Attachment*. London: Hogarth Press.

Bratman, S. & Knight, D. (2004). *Health Food Junkies: Orthorexia Nervosa—the Health Food Eating Disorder*. New York: Broadway Books.

Decety, J. & Meltzoff, A. N. (2011). Empathy, imitation, and the social brain. In A. Copland & P. Goldie (eds), *Empathy: Philosophical and Psychological Perspectives*. New York: Oxford University Press. pp. 58–81.

American Psychiatric Association. (2000). *Diagnostic and Statistical Manual of Mental Disorders* (4th edn). Washington, DC: Author.

American Psychiatric Association. (2013). *Diagnostic and Statistical Manual of Mental Disorders* (5th edn). Washington, DC: Author.

Eigen, M. (2005). *Emotional Storm*. Middletown, CT: Wesleyan University Press.

Fonagy, P. & Target, M. (1997). Attachment and reflective function: Their role in self-organization. *Development and Psychopathology*, 9: 679–700.

Fonagy, P., Target, M., & Gergely, G. (2000). Attachment and borderline personality disorder: A theory and some evidence. *Psychiatric Clinics of North America*, 23(1): 103–122.

Freud, S. (1925). Negation. *Standard Edition*. London: The Hogarth Press, 19: 3–66.

Greenspan, S. & Wieder, S. (1998). *The Child with Special Needs: Encouraging Intellectual and Emotional Growth*. Reading, MA: Perseus Books.

Hebb, D. O. (1949). *The Organization of Behavior: A Neuropsychological Theory*. New York: Wiley.

Hesse, E. & Main, M. (2000). Disorganized infant, child, and adult attachment: Collapse in behavioral and attentional strategies. *Journal of the American Psychoanalytic Association*, 8(4): 1099–1127.

Hofer, M. A. (1990). Early symbiotic processes: Hard evidence from a soft place. In A. Glick & S. Bone (eds), *Pleasure Beyond the Pleasure Principle*. New Haven, CT: Yale University Press. pp. 55–78.

Johnson, C. & Connors, M. (1987). *The Etiology and Treatment of Bulimia Nervosa: A Biopsychosocial Perspective*. New York: Basic Books.

Kotulak, R. (1996). *Inside the Brain: Revolutionary Discoveries of How the Mind Works*. Kansas City, MO: Andrews McMeel.

Kullman, A. (1995). *The 'Autizoid' Personality and the Eating Disorder*. Ph.D. (unpublished). Newport Psychoanalytic Institute, Tustin, CA.

—— (2007). The 'perseverant' personality: A pre-attachment perspective on the etiology and evolution of binge-purge eating disorders. *Psychoanalytic Dialogues*, 17(5): 705–732.

LeDoux, J. (1996). *The Emotional Brain: The Mysterious Underpinnings of Emotional Life*. New York: Simon and Schuster.

—— (2002). *Synaptic Self: How Our Brains Become Who We Are*. New York: Viking.

Lemche, E., Klann-Delius, G., Koch, R., & Joraschky, P. (2004). Mentalizing language development in a longitudinal attachment sample: Implications for alexithymia. *Psychotherapy and Psychosomatics*, 73(6): 366–374.

Main, M. (2000). The organized categories of infant, child, and adult attachment: Flexible vs. inflexible attention under attachment-related stress. *Journal of the American Psychoanalytic Association*, 48(4): 1055–1096.

McDougall, J. (1989). *Theaters of the Body: A Psychoanalytic Approach to Psychosomatic Illness*. New York: W. W. Norton.

Ogden, T. H. (1994). The analytic third: Working with intersubjective clinical facts. *International Journal of Psychoanalysis*, 75: 3–19.

Perry, B. D., Pollard, R. A., Blakely, T. L., Baker, W. L., & Vigilante, D. (1995). Childhood trauma, the neurobiology of adaptation, and 'use-dependent' development of the brain: How states become traits. *Infant Mental Health Journal*, 16: 271–291.

*Random House Webster's College Dictionary* (1992). New York: Random House.

Schore, A. N. (1994). *Affect Regulation and the Origin of the Self: The Neurobiology of Emotional Development*. Hillsdale, NJ: Lawrence Erlbaum.

——— (2001). Effects of a secure attachment relationship on right brain development, affect regulation, and infant mental health. *Infant Mental Health Journal*, 22(1–2): 7–66.

Siegel, D. (1999). *The Developing Mind—Toward a Neurobiology of Interpersonal Experience*. New York: Guilford Press.

Sifneos, P. E. (1973). The prevalence of 'alexithymic' characteristics in psychosomatic patients. *Psychotherapy and Psychosomatics*, 22(2): 255–26.

Sroufe, L. A., Carlson, E. A., Levy, A. K., & Egeland, B. (1999). Implications of attachment theory for developmental psychopathology. *Development & Psychopathology*, 11: 1–13.

Stern, D. (1983). The early differentiation of self and other. In S. Kaplan & J. D. Lichtenberg (eds), *Reflections on Self-Psychology*. Hillsdale, NJ: Analytic Press.

——— (1985). *The Interpersonal World of the Infant*. New York: Basic Books.

Tallal, P., Merzenich, M., Miller, S., & Jenkins, W. (1998). Language learning impairments: Integrating basic science, technology and remediation. *Experimental Brain Research*, 123: 210–219.

Tronick, E. Z. (1989). Emotions and emotional communication in infants. *Psychologist*, 44: 112–119.

Watillon-Naveau, A. (1992). Alice or the vicissitudes of the mother-daughter relationship. *International Review of Psychoanalysis*, 19: 209–216.

Winnicott, D. W. (1958). The capacity to be alone. *International Journal of Psychoanalysis*, 39: 416–420.

——— (1968). The use of an object and relating through identifications. In *Playing and Reality*. London: Tavistock, 1971, pp. 86–94.

——— (1971). Mirror-role of mother and family in child development. In *Playing and Reality*. London: Tavistock, pp. 111–118.

——— (1974). Fear of breakdown. *International Review of Psychoanalysis*, 1: 103–107.

# acknowledgements

To W. R. Bion, M.D., whose extraordinary genius has had a profound influence on the foundations of my thinking;

To Michael Eigen, Ph.D, whose genius, generosity, and unflagging support have honored me and infused my thinking with heart, soul, and spirit;

To my dear friends, mentors, colleagues, publisher, and editors, many of whom have encouraged this project from its inception and endured through the many winters and springs it has taken to bring it to fruition;

To Gwyn and Gabi for their love, friendship, and incalculable efforts in preparing this manuscript;

To my patients, who have reached out for connection and touched my soul in ways big and small, beyond words;

To my beloved husband and family, whose love and support have sustained and nurtured me in every way and at every turn. My eternal love and gratitude.

# index